Going for a Song:
English Furniture

Going for a Song: English Furniture

Arthur Negus talks to Max Robertson

Edited by Max Robertson

British Broadcasting Corporation

Published by the British Broadcasting Corporation
35 Marylebone High Street, London W.1

First Published 1969, Reprinted 1969 (twice)
© Arthur Negus 1969
SBN 563 08322 0

Printed in England by Jolly and Barber Ltd, Rugby

Contents

Plates

We would like to thank Bruton, Knowles & Co., of
Gloucester, and the Radio Times Hulton Picture library
for permission to reproduce photographs.

The BBC would like to thank Bruton, Knowles and Co.,
and John Irving for their help in the production of the book.

Foreword

When some four years ago I was fortunate enough to become the Chairman of *Going for a Song* Arthur Negus had already established himself as the Familiar of the programme and of a rapidly growing number of viewers. You can imagine how grateful I was to have him as a sheet anchor – this man who could talk not only interestingly and usually extremely knowledge-ably, but also with such a homely personality that I consider he is one of the greatest gifts to Television since Gilbert Harding.

Since those early days Arthur has endeared himself to millions who think of him as the last word on 'antiquity'. He would be the first to deny this, for, of course, it is an impossibility. But as you well know he has an incredibly wide knowledge of antiques in general and of furniture in particular. Not for nothing has he been called Willie Woodworm and to watch him turn a piece of furniture upside down, investigate its antecedents and almost unerringly find any bar sinister on its escutcheon, is at once an education and entertainment.

John Irving, the first producer of *Going for a Song*, suggested to Arthur that he should write a book, to be edited by Irving, that would preserve some of what he had said on the programme. After some persuasion Arthur agreed, but John then left Bristol to take up an appointment in America. I shall always be grateful that he then suggested I should become Arthur's editor. I found myself eager and fearful – eager to hear the Arthurian legend but fearful lest, by any clumsiness of editing or pretence of literary awareness, I might destroy the essential Arthur, the man who talks so naturally to the family circle.

It was eventually done in several sessions with a portable tape recorder. Arthur talked to – and occasionally was prompted by – me or Tony Kingsford, the BBC's Books Editor, who sat in too. He talked sometimes at his home in Cheltenham, once in an old house whose contents he was cataloguing, once in the house of a dealer friend (the one mentioned on page 28) and once or twice at my home.

11

This was all transcribed and then began my main labour of editing, correcting, regrouping—all the while hearing Arthur's voice and trying to ensure that his distinctive phraseology and natural gift for telling essentials were not blurred or emaciated by any pernickety alteration for the sake of so-called style. On occasions I even had to overrule Arthur whose new-found sense of authorship prompted him to want higher literary flights.

So if I can claim any credit in this book, besides that of a catalyst for Arthur's thoughts, it is that you will find him preserved as you know him. As you read I hope you will be listening to the familiar voice and absorbing the Negus of knowledge on antique furniture that is Arthur.

First we meet him and discover his fascinating background which explains the man and how he gained his knowledge. Then he gives us a general introduction to period English Furniture. He follows by discussing, in illustrated detail and by subjects, pieces he has known and liked—with particular reference to several we have shown on 'Going for a Song'. Finally he has added various appendices, abbreviated hints on style, value and period identification, that you will find very useful for quick reference.

Arthur hopes you will enjoy his book but above all that you will profit by it. If you do it will make him very happy.

Max Robertson

How it all began

I'm often asked as I go about the country, 'How did all this start? Where did you pick up this knowledge?' and I always tell people much the same story, which is the truth. I learnt it by leaving school at the age of seventeen and going on the bench with my father. He was a cabinet-maker pure and simple. He had a shop in Reading with some antique furniture in it, but his only interest really was in the workshop behind, and he was a very, very good cabinet-maker.

Going on the bench – that meant to say standing by his side, never being allowed to touch any tools. 'Put those down,' he used to say, 'look, watch me. This is how you sharpen a scraper, this is how you set a plane. You can always tell if a man is a good cabinet-maker if you give him a scraper to sharpen. Get under that table, can't you see that's been made from a washstand? Look at this drawer, they never made drawers like that in the Eighteenth century, this is a very late, modern way of making a drawer.'

'Do this, do that, get under there, can't you see this – I shall never get any sense into you.' And in ten months he died. So there we found ourselves with a shop with a few bits of furniture in it – a workshop absolutely choc-a-bloc with work, and, for the first time, a cheque-book. Oh I wished someone would come in so that I could write a cheque. And soon a man came in wanting me to buy a table. So off we went down to his house.

'Would you buy this table?'–'Yes'–'What would you give for it?'–
'Fifteen pounds'–'I'll take that'.

So I wrote out the cheque and carried the table back. I put it in the shop,
went up the stairs to my mother, fetched her down. 'Look at this table.
You see, this is what we want to do. I don't want to spend all my life in
this workshop. What I'd like to do is to go out and buy tables like this.
Now look at this table, it only costs fifteen pounds. You just wait and see
what we get for it.' Well she did, she waited and waited. It took seven
years for us to get one pound for it. But you see, this is the way that people
buy their knowledge. I learnt an awful lot about that table and this was
one thing I stuck in the back of my mind – never to give any serious money
for that type of table.

Then of course I went up to London to the London salerooms. For seventeen shillings I made a great purchase – fifty-six pounds weight of Georgian
copper pennies. You will recall they are those round thick pennies, which
are known in the trade as Cartwheels. Well for seventeen shillings I
bought fifty-six pounds weight of them, some few hundred no doubt. I
carried them all across London, back to the train, back to the shop. Not so
bad this time, because it took me about five days to discover that I'd
bought exactly seventeen shillings worth of scrap metal. They were, in
fact, worth nothing as coins. That lesson cost me next to nothing, and it
taught me still a bit more.

And then I recall going to a sale at Goring near Henley and for seventeen
shillings, at a little tiny country sale, buying a glass cake-dish. I brought it
back, of course, gave it to my mother who washed it and she said – 'I can't
understand why you buy things like this. Look at this cake dish!' Every
time it was wetted it went absolutely white. She said, 'You see, you can't
even wash the thing. No one will ever buy this.' Anyway it was marked
30/– and got left in the back of the shop, because neither of us had any
hope of selling it, until one day it suddenly went. Someone gave the 30/–
for it simply because they recognised it as a piece of Ravenscroft glass.
So, for those of you who don't know, George Ravenscroft (1618–81) was
a very early maker of lead or 'flint' glass. He had a little glass-works at
Henley-on-Thames, probably only a shed, and this undoubtedly was a
piece of Ravenscroft glass, of course the only piece I've ever had, the
only piece I'm ever likely to have. When I tell you that a Ravenscroft

goblet sold at Sotheby's a year ago for two thousand pounds you must feel that we didn't overcharge our client when we managed to get thirty shillings out of him.

This business of the glass going white is a thing that happens to early glass, because this was soda glass, not glass made from flints. It has this peculiarity that it does tend to go very milky and very, very cloudy when wet. Of course, as it dries off and dries out so the glass becomes clear. But there's another thing, another bit of knowledge learnt the hard way by experience, and I might say I've been looking for a piece of Ravenscroft glass ever since. And of course I shan't find one now.

Then I bought a clock, a grandfather clock. I was taken to a house by a runner and eventually bought, for £25, a grandfather clock in a deal case. I didn't realise it was a pine case until I got home and I thought, Oh dear, what a fool I've been again. This clock can't be worth this money. But a man came into the shop and said 'How much for the grandfather?' And I was so anxious to sell it to him that I said, '£27 10s.' and, to my amazement, he said, 'I'll have it.' And I was absolutely delighted until I was told some years after, when I recalled this and that the name on the dial was East, that Edward East was one of the eight most prominent clock-makers ever to have lived in England. And of course it didn't matter two hoots whether the case was in deal, or paper for that matter, the movement itself was, even in those days, worth a hundred or two. And there was I absolutely delighted to take fifty bob profit out of an Edward East grandfather, simply because East meant nothing to me. I suppose that grandfather today, even still in its ebonised pine case, would make in the region of £2,000.

And this is how you go on. You gradually learn. I mean, clock-makers' names on clock movements meant nothing to me when I was twenty-four or twenty-five, but in time you find out and you keep your eyes and ears open. You see a man suddenly giving a hundred pounds for something, which you don't understand, so then you look and you see it's got a name and so then you remember to memorise certain names. Names like Tompion and Knibb, of course, are so famous that they don't need memorising, but there are many, many other fine makers whose clocks make money simply because they were superb early Eighteenth- or late Seventeenth-century makers. Even all through their experimental times with pendulums and one thing and the other, their pieces all make money solely

15

because of their names and the quality of the clocks.

So you see how you gradually go on from tables to clocks to pieces of glass and of course you go to sales. I don't know whether everyone reading this book realises it, but an auction sale is one of the cleverest concocted affairs that anyone could ever possibly imagine. You know there are four or five different strata of dealers at every sale. There are the tip-top sort of people from London or from other big cities who might visit a good sale, and then there are the local, very good men, and other very good men from towns up to a hundred or even two hundred miles away. Then there are lesser dealers and also people in their early days, exactly like I was, virtually on the floor, going to sales to gain knowledge, going to sales to watch and see what happens.

And I wonder how many people realise that often at a country house sale a fellow–perhaps sitting on a wall eating some strawberries, with a nice boater on his head and paying not the slightest interest in anything– is probably the man in complete charge of everything that might be going on inside where the actual goods are being sold. Well, I went to sales and none of these dealers on the higher rungs of the ladder, of course, recognised me. No one even spoke to me until one day one of the men, who I knew to be very high up the ladder, suddenly said to me, 'Good morning,' and I said, 'Good morning, sir.' I thought, Oh recognition at last!

'You've got that little shop in Reading, haven't you,' he said. And I said 'Yes'. 'Ah,' he said, 'I've often looked through the window. I haven't been in yet, I must come in and see if you've got anything to suit me.' 'Thank you very much.' He said, 'I wonder if you'd like to take a share in something I'm going to buy at this sale.' I said, 'Yes I would–what is it?' 'Oh,' he said, 'you'll know what it is. It's going to make a lot of money! You'll soon know what it is as soon as I buy it.' I said, 'Yes, thank you very much for asking me, I'd very much like to be in this.' And of course you can imagine I went all around this house looking for something going to make a lot of money. I couldn't see anything.

Anyway I waited, the sale started, nothing seemed to happen except this fellow came back to me and said, 'You might like to know there are seven of us now in this. I've got six other people in this and myself and so there's seven of us.' I said, 'You haven't bought it yet?' 'No, no, no–oh no,' he said, 'you'll know, it'll cost a lot of money.' So I waited and he started bidding and then he became the owner of a marble bust for two hundred guineas. £210 for a white marble bust of a man. This meant nothing to me at all, but I wrote a cheque out for £30 and took it to him and gave it to him. He said, 'Thanks very much, would you mind clearing it?' I said, 'Clear it?' 'Yes,' he said, 'take it away, take it home, you won't have it a minute, I shall sell it overnight, but will you clear it?' I said, 'Yes I'll clear it.'

So with some help I got it onto the back of a little car I had and took it to my shop in Reading. My wife and I struggled with this blessed marble bust. I know for certain she was frightened to death of it. Anyway we didn't know where to put it for safety, for to us £200 was such a lot of money. As I say, we didn't know where to put it so, as we had to be very careful with it, we laid it in the middle of a spare-room bed. This thing lay in state in this bed and I know all the while we had it I'm certain sure my wife never opened the door to go in. I had a peep every now and then, but there it rested and I should think a month or six weeks went by and not a soul came anywhere near us.

And then this man appeared and he said, 'Bad job about the bust.' 'Oh,' I said, 'is it?' 'Oh yes,' he said, 'that was a very bad job.' 'What's happened then?' 'Oh,' he said, 'I haven't sold it, you see. You would have thought that such a lovely article as that would have sold in a moment but,' he said, 'I don't know, I haven't been able to sell it. Something's gone wrong. But this is the first deal that you and I have had together and you're not very old and I wouldn't like to see you lose any money. I suggest now that you let me give you your £30 back.' I would willingly have taken it except that I thought, 'Well it's no good showing the white flag, he'll never ask me again.' So I put on a brave front and said, 'Oh no, of course not, no matter what happens I'll still stick. Perhaps it'll be all right.' 'Oh well,' he said, 'we'll do our best, but I thought I'd better offer you – thank you very much.' And off he went.

But I discovered that he was visiting all the six participants and of the six he managed to buy four shares for the £30 each that they'd cost. So now the position was simply that I still had an interest in this bust, another man had an interest in this bust who was twice my age, and of course the man himself – three of us. He soon came back after this first visit and said 'I've sold the bust.' 'Oh,' I said, 'good.' 'Yes,' he said, 'and it shows you a

17

fiver profit, I'm so pleased.' I said, 'So am I.' And he gave me the £35 and took the bust away.

That I thought was the end of it until I met the second dealer some months later. He inquired of me, 'Has so-and-so ever paid up over the bust?' 'Oh yes,' I said, 'a long time ago. He gave me a fiver.' 'Oh,' he said, 'you were silly. He came to me with that tale and I told him what he could do with the fiver, so he gave me £15.' So you see here was a nice position. I got a fiver, the other man got £15, the bust now stands in the forecourt of a museum in America and we've no idea and probably never shall know what it did realise when he sold it. The bust was reputed to be, and so far as I know still is, one of the few authentic busts of William Penn.

Of course there are dealers and dealers – as you find in all walks of life. For most I have a high regard. I don't paint them black like so many people seem to. You see it has to be borne in mind that they find themselves in many rather awkward predicaments. For example, this happened to me and as a result of it I said I would never again make anybody an offer for anything in a house. This concerned going to a house in Reading, a very, very poor house. I don't think I've ever been in a poorer. There was absolutely nothing in this house. There were two or three little mites running about the place with hardly any clothes on and a woman, bedraggled, saying, 'Oh do please try and buy something.'

And in all this confusion and dirt there was a famille rose plate, an ordinary nine-inch famille rose plate, hanging on the wall–and this, mark you, was 35 years ago. I said 'Well, you really have nothing.' 'Oh,' she said, 'are you sure you've had a look round? Have you been everywhere?' I said, 'Yes I've been everywhere. There is just one plate hanging up on that wall. I wouldn't mind buying that.' So she said, 'Well, I'll sell that. What will you give me for it?' And I thought, now what on earth shall I bid this woman? I said, 'I'll give you £5 for this plate,' and this was absolutely every penny that it was worth. She said, 'Oh well, I'll let you know in the morning.' I said, 'All right.'

In the morning, a man who was in a smaller way of business than myself – and goodness knows, that was small enough – phoned me up. I used to buy all the things that this man took in. He rang me up and he said, 'I've bought a famille rose plate.' 'Ah', I said, 'I know where you bought this from,' and I told him the address. 'That's quite right,' he said, 'a woman

18

came into the shop with it under her arm, and I said, "How much do you want for that?" She said, "I will take five guineas for it. I've been offered five pounds by Mr So-and-So." So I bought it. Is it any good?' I said, 'Well, I shall have to buy it off you, of course,' but honestly, it wasn't worth more than a fiver.

But that lesson went home to me, because I was absolutely convinced if I'd said to this woman, 'Well, you've got a plate there on that wall, of course it's no good, but I'll give you 10/– for it,' she would have jumped at it. Because I bid £5 (a lot of money in those days, I expect, to her) which was a very fair price to give for a famille rose plate – they're worth more today of course, but that was a fair price then – she whipped it into another shop and asked five guineas. I had to give him 10/– profit on it because it was my custom to buy all he bought. I don't remember what happened to the plate except we probably got the money back or very near it.

But you see, you don't hear this side of dealers' stories. You don't hear the hundred and one times that people walk into a shop with a piece of blue and white oriental porcelain, about which they know nothing, and say, 'We're going off to Canada in three weeks' time. We believe this to be very old. What will you give us for it?' Now, the dealer has this said to him at least three times a week. He knows jolly well the people are going nowhere. He knows he's going to do a free valuation on this piece of blue and white, and this is why, in many instances, jolly good dealers are absolutely spoilt because they are taken advantage of in this way.

Of course, there's always a correct and proper way in which an owner can find out exactly what his things are worth. If he walks into any reputable dealer and says, 'I have a piece of blue and white porcelain. I know nothing of it. Would you for a fee tell me exactly what it is and what its value is?', I'm absolutely certain that the owner would be told and given a fair and honest appraisal of that particular thing. But some people just walk in and think they're so clever that they can catch a dealer like this. They don't realise this happens to every dealer hundreds and hundreds of times in his years of dealing, so quite rightly he absolutely refuses to make any comment and will rather tend to be offhand and tie the owner down by saying, 'If you don't know what you want for it, I'm afraid you must take it somewhere else.'

And of course there are always those kind of people who go to an auction

sale and watch Mr A or Mr B and, if either of these two very well-known
dealers can bid £100 for an article, they for their part think they are clever
if they buy it for £110. Now this is a true story. I used to go to sales around
Reading as a dealer and got to know other bigger important dealers. At a
sale at a well-known house just outside Reading fifty or a hundred London
dealers arrived at this country mansion. A lot of very fine things there, and
it was well known around Reading at that time that there was a gentleman
who used to turn up at such sales and always run the trade. This means to
say that he'd seem to take great pleasure, if he saw dealer A or B bidding,
in immediately starting to bid and run them along a little bit. And invariably he would always end up by buying the best lot, so much so that
often when I saw this man come to a sale, I used to turn round and get on
my bicycle and cycle home, because I knew there was just going to be a
pantomime again. This chap was going to bid like billy-o and would buy
the best lots and it would be impossible for a chap like me to buy anything.

Now at this important sale, this man turned up. And I can assure you
that forty years ago auctioneers religiously took 5% increase on the last bid.
A fine table turned up and the auctioneer asked for a starting bid of 30/–.
A man whom I knew well as one of the leading London dealers raised his
thumb, and 'Thank you, sir – 30/– I'm bid,' said the auctioneer when this
other man, who was well-known to him and to everybody of course,
immediately raised his catalogue. 31/6, 34/–, 36/6, 38/–, two pounds – this
was how it went – two guineas, £2 4s., £2 6s., £2 8s., and so on, both
people bidding ding-dong.

Then two or three Londoners walked behind the dealer who was bidding
and just sort of gave him a nudge, which he well understood as meaning
that he was to make this man pay for this article if he was going to buy it.
In other words, he could bid well over the odds for it and they would take
their full share of any loss which might be incurred. Eventually one
thousand pounds was bid by the dealer, then a thousand guineas by the
gentleman. Everyone was silent. The gentleman became the owner of the
table at a thousand guineas. No one said a word. No one passed any comment. The sale went on and eventually everybody disappeared and that,
so far as I thought, was the end of the table.

But seven years or so later I went to the sale of this gentleman's effects.
He had died. A local firm was selling the remaining contents of his house.

I went and viewed it and as you may have been thinking I recognised the table. I thought, Good Lord, there's that thousand pound table standing there. So I said nothing to anybody but went along to the auction and I became the proud owner of this table for £50. I took it back to the shop and I really thought I'd made my fortune. I tried to sell it to all sorts of people and eventually, after about nine months, I got a fiver profit. Now this is the extent to which dealers will go to protect their own interests if they're upset or annoyed by a man who deliberately goes to every sale to try and get the better of them.

I saw a funny thing happen at another sale I attended. This sale was well on the way and so was a fellow who was attending it: well, he daren't have breathed into one of these modern breathalysers because it would have turned green immediately. He'd certainly been waiting for something to come up in the sale, and been waiting at the local hotel and had imbibed rather too freely. He came in and he stood right at the end of the rostrum, and he stood there gazing up at the auctioneer, who was just going to start selling the linen.

The first lot of linen came along and this fellow said £4 and of course no one else bid because it was too much. It was knocked down to him and, come the next lot of linen, '£4' he said. He bought the first four or five lots of linen like this – £4 a time, nothing more, nothing less. And then another lot came up. '£4', he said and the auctioneer took no notice, saying '30/- I'm bid . . . 35 . . . 35 . . . £2 . . . £2.' This fellow interrupted and said, 'Look here, are you refusing to take my bid?' So the auctioneer said, 'No, if you will be so foolish, of course I'll take your bid. What are you bidding?' He said, '£4', so this again was knocked down. But the auctioneer turned to me and he said, 'I think it'd be as well if you sent a boy down to the local police station. Tell him we're in no trouble but we might be in a little difficulty sooner or later. We've got a chap here who's been celebrating a bit, who's just buying every lot, so perhaps he'd have a walk up in case.'

So off went the boy and when he got back he came up to me and I said, 'Well, where's the policeman?' 'Oh,' he said, 'I went to the police house and I rang the bell and a lady opened the door and I told her what trouble we were in at the sale and she said, 'Well, I'm sorry but we don't open before six o'clock!' Now this is an extraordinary thing to put down in print but I can vouch for every word. It's absolutely true. So we were stuck with

21

this good fellow who did in fact buy every lot of linen – about 50 or 60 lots all told. He bought every single lot but when the linen was over, he'd finished. He pulled a cheque-book out of his pocket and wrote the cheque. He wasn't allowed to take anything away of course, not until the end of the sale, by which time he'd sobered up a bit.

He produced a smallish car, which became absolutely filled with bolsters and pillows and eiderdowns and everything under the sun. He had to go home and come back for another load and on his second visit, the head porter said to him, 'You had a pretty good day.' 'Ah yes,' he said. 'Of course I made a mistake, because my wife sent me down here and I went into the local because I'd got to the sale much too early. I had one or two and when I got to the sale, I couldn't for the life of me remember what I had been told to buy, although I knew it was some linen, and I ended up by buying the lot and in fact all my wife wanted was a few towels.'

There are some funny things that happen, you know, when you visit houses. Invariably the house you visit with bated breath, because the owner has written you a letter in which he says that everything is supreme, turns out to be disappointing. Whereas oft-times one goes into an ordinary house, where some of the nicest things are discovered, perhaps not thought much of and even uncared for by the owner. I remember once going into a house and a gentleman showed me some pieces of silver. I was very pleased to take them away to include in a sale, when he suddenly said, 'Oh, I've got a clock if only I could find it. I wonder if you can sell that.' So I said, 'Well, I'll have a look at it.'

He eventually found this clock under a heap of clothes in an old cloak-room, and he brought it out and I said, 'My word, that's rather nice.' 'Rather nice,' he said, 'I've been trying to sell it for years. I offered it to a man for £25. He wouldn't buy it.' 'Well,' I said, 'I should like to sell this. As a matter of fact I don't think I dare sell it.' 'Why not?' he asked. I said, 'It's gold.' 'What!' And it was. It was in fact a tiny mantel-clock, a tiny Eighteenth-century mantel-clock made in gold. And I didn't sell it. I took it away and I sent it to Christie's. It brought about £780. And when I think how this was in fact offered for £25 to someone who came to the door and that he refused to buy it because he thought it was brass, I just wonder what he might feel like if he reads this book.

You might well wonder why I thought this thing was gold. And I couldn't really be certain, because obviously one can't carry acid to test gold. But this is this sort of flair again. This thing was in the prettiest Eighteenth-century shaped, miniature rococo case you could imagine. And I just took a chance. But of course when I tested it with acid it was gold. It's the outline of these things that tells you about them.

You see, I'm often sent photographs of pieces of furniture or pieces of silver or plate which have an art nouveau outline. And of course there is always the little bit of family history on the bottom whereby the correspondent knows this has been handed down since Charles II's reign. It might be silver, but there it is – art nouveau. The things of any period carry a certain outline. And if you have a clock, we'll say, the outline of which is very, very definitely art nouveau circa 1900, say from Liberty's, how one can associate such a design with a Carolean design completely defeats me. But without this sort of feeling, without this flair, without this something – call it what you will – it must be very difficult.

Many people have this flair because many people can go into a house, with no idea what they are looking at, and say, 'Well, that was a pretty chair by the fire, wasn't it?' They might be completely ignorant of any period or age but usually such a chair, which is spoken of in that manner, is an old one. Maybe it's because of its outline, maybe because of its overall quality, maybe the colour, maybe something. But perhaps if we call it the attractiveness of it, that's what impresses itself on someone's mind so that they remember it and say, 'That chair in that house, that looked nice to me.'

It's a remarkable thing, but there is in England a mass of furniture which is genuinely old, and when it emerges from a home for the first time, practically everybody with knowledge says, 'Well, what a nice old family thing this looks.' For some reason people can tell a piece which is fresh out of a home for the first time from an article that may have appeared four or five times in London sale-rooms. It could still be a good article, but there is just this difference.

This is the moment to tell you a story about a dealer friend of mine, with whom I went to a sale one day. He had a flair and a sixth sense about good pieces if anyone did. I don't know whether you'll believe me when I say that certain dealers have only to appear at a sale for the value of the things to go up considerably in other people's minds. In other words, if a man is known to be say the 'king of oak', he has only to appear at a sale where there might be a fine piece of oak, for this particular article to become much more valuable in the eyes of certain other dealers who might be present.

Well, we went to a sale one day and there was no one there of any particular moment. And there sticking out of a pile of bits of furniture – you know how they used to be stacked up in local country auctions – one could just see the base of a cabriole leg. What it belonged to no one had any idea. My friend knew full well that if he went and started pulling this stack about, this would probably cost him £50 or £100 more because so many eyes would be on him and would watch him looking at it. So he walked straight past this table, and we went and stood at the back of the room. He knew that if he paid too much attention to it he might not even end up being its owner.

At this stage he still didn't know what it was. But he went to a local dealer, a little village dealer, and said, 'I've got a little interest in a table up there. It is a table, isn't it?' And the chap said, 'Oh yes, that one on the cabriole leg?' 'Yes,' he said, 'that's the one. I wonder if you'd do something for me. I shall stop about at this sale but I shan't take the slightest interest in this table. Whatever it makes, you take particular care that you hold it.' There was no question of how much money.

So it eventually comes up for sale and one can see it's a table. We go nowhere near it at all and this man who has been commissioned to do this deed, buys it for £35. So he gave the little dealer a cheque for £35 and a fiver for his trouble. When I tell you that that table is one that the Victoria and Albert Museum possesses to this very day, you can perhaps understand how this man felt all the while this was going on, knowing he had no control over what took place, apart from saying to a man, 'Whatever happens, that table is to come out and be mine'.

That man, of course, knew exactly what he was doing and knew a good thing when he saw it. He puts me in mind of another man who clearly didn't. A few years ago I was called to a house by a gentleman who said, 'Come and see what my daughter-in-law is doing to my home'. He told me no more than this over the telephone. So I went to his house and met him and his daughter-in-law. She had simply been upstairs in the maids' bedrooms and the attics and begun bringing downstairs the original furnishings of the house. In Victorian times the chairs had all been poked upstairs to make way for new Victorian chairs, new dining-tables, Victorian library armchairs in oak, whilst upstairs in the attics were languishing all the lovely period furnishings of the house. And this gentleman fetched me because he said, 'My daughter-in-law will listen to you so please tell her to stop it. This lovely furniture, which I bought myself thirty or forty years ago, she wants to sell.' And of course I had rather a difficult task because my sympathies were entirely with the daughter-in-law.

We once had a sale in Wales and a man came and shook hands with me and I said, 'What on earth are you doing here?' And he said, 'Well, London is so hot and sticky that I decided to come out of it for the duration of this sale of yours. Where are you stopping?' I told him and he decided to stop in the same hotel with me. Now this is a man who is in the habit of visiting Christie's and Sotheby's and paying anything up to two, three, four, even five thousand for any lot that he fancies.

I said to him at dinner the first night, 'You must have had some luck when you started.' And he said, 'Luck, I never had any luck in my life.' And that was the end of that, but the next night at dinner he said, 'I've been thinking of what you said, perhaps I did have a bit of luck.' And he went on to tell me about it. His father died just prior to the 1914 war. They were in the East End of London, in a small shop, as poor as church mice. They had the word 'China' over the door.

He said, 'We had no idea where the next penny was coming from and the stock consisted of only three or four broken sets of toilet ware – when a man came in and said, "Do you buy china?" And I said, "Yes, have you got some for sale?" The man said, "Yes I have." "What have you got?" "Egg-cups." "How many?" "Thousands," he said. I enquired further and he said that a boat had just put into London docks and had dumped on the side of the wharf five of the biggest crates of egg-cups he could imagine. The man, because war was imminent, had jumped back on the boat and had said to Taffy, if you can flog those you may do so, I'm off back. And he'd gone. "So if you'd like to go down to London docks and find this man Taffy you can buy them."

'Off I went. I bought them eventually from him for thirty shillings a crate.' He went on then to describe how his troubles really began from the moment when they were delivered outside his shop. These enormous crates of egg-cups wouldn't go through the shop door, they had to stand on the pavement. Then the police came and made him move them and they were dumped in a pub yard close by. He unpacked them, thousands and thousands of egg-cups. Penny each, two a penny, three a penny. He swears to this day that everyone in the East End of London has got egg-cups.

'But,' he said, 'we made a profit, nothing very wonderful, but we got rid of thousands of them and only had one crate left. I was sick of them so I rang up a man, a friend of mine, miles out of London and suggested he might take this last crate of egg-cups. He agreed to take them for a nominal price but said, "Don't send those large crates down to me, I've seen them. You must unpack them and put them in decent cartons." So we unpacked the last crate which I sold to him.

'In the middle of this last crate were twelve pairs of Meissen figures. I immediately went into the shop, threw out the egg-cups and the toilet ware, and put eleven pairs of figures in the window. One pair I've got to this day. Eleven pairs I marked up £10 and £12 a pair. They sold in a moment. With that money I began immediately going to Christie's and Sotheby's. I bought a little pair of figures for £4, for £8, for £12, for £20 and this is how I started. So perhaps I did have a bit of luck.'

I said there were good and bad dealers. Well, I'll tell you a story now about a good one. I was asked to go and see some furniture in a house in Norfolk and when I got there, I discovered a nice house with a lady and a gentleman living in it, the gentleman being blind. And this lady explained to me that she wanted me to walk round the house to see if I could find something worth £500 or £600 that would enable her husband to have an operation. And so I said, 'Yes, I'll have a walk round.' So I walked round, going into every room, and apart from there being some nice things worth thirties and forties and fifties, there was no one thing of anything like five or six hundred pounds value.

So this I told her and said how sorry I was, but that in point of fact there was nothing there that would produce that money, unless she wanted to sell a number of things. No, she didn't want to do that, and her husband, who was, I must say, one of the most cheerful fellows I've ever met, shouted out, 'Did you show Mr Negus the cabinet?' She said, 'No.' 'Well,' he said, 'you're not committed to those auctioneers, are you?' She said, 'Oh no, no, no. They've only said what they would do with it.' 'Show it to Mr Negus.'

I was then taken into a small room which I'd not been in before and shown the cabinet which is illustrated here in plate *1*. 'Oh,' I said, 'now this is a very different thing.' You can see what a magnificent little secretaire-cabinet this is. You notice the serpentine front, the serpentine end, pure Hepplewhite. There's a very deep fitted drawer on the top, fitted as a secretaire. The flap falls down. All those peculiar shapes. Absolutely George Hepplewhite at his very best, inlaid with those beautiful ovals, a lovely bit of English cabinet-making. I am sure you can see from the illustration the supreme quality of the wood and veneers used.

I said to this woman, 'Now this, you're all right with this. If I were to send a man back here would you have pluck enough to ask him £750 for it?' And to my amazement she said, 'No.' I said, 'Why not?' 'Oh no,' she said, 'I couldn't do that. You see this fellow said it's worth £150.' I said, 'Well, I don't mind that. Do you mean to say if I sent a man here and told him you'd got a fine Hepplewhite cabinet you wouldn't ask him £750?' She said, 'No, I'd rather not.' So I said, 'I'll bring him myself.'

So I rang a friend of mine and I said we had to go to Norfolk the next week-end, and he said, 'I don't want to go to Norfolk.' 'But,' I said, 'this is a lovely bit of furniture. It's £750.' Then he said, 'You go and buy it for me.' I said, 'No, I shan't do that. You come and see it.' Well it ended by my picking him up, and driving his car up to Norfolk.

In we went and were shown the cabinet. Of course my friend liked it. 'But,' he said, '£750 is too dear, you know.' I said, 'What are you talking about? This poor fellow is blind. How much too dear is it?' And he said '£50.' I said, 'Don't be silly.' So he said, 'All right, well then give her the money, but I shall never sell it.' And for many years I visited his house and in his drawing-room there always stood this cabinet.

It just shows you that it's not always the making of money which attracts people to being antique dealers. Here was a man who had no great pleasure in making a profit in that sense. Of course he had to buy and sell things and make profits to live, but he was just as happy buying that one cabinet and never selling it. He has since died and the cabinet is still in the same room and I don't suppose his widow will ever sell it either.

So it just goes to prove there is this type of man and he is not the only one by any means who is quite content to sit and look at a nice article rather than to have it pass through his hands and say, 'Oh, I made £100, I made £200 out of this'. The position dealers find themselves in today often seems foolish, in so far as they perhaps buy an article—let's say a pair of Georgian silver sauce-boats for example. They buy a pair of sauce-boats, they keep them in their shop for six months, looking at them, enjoying them, not minding. Then eventually they sell them. They sell the pair for £350 and then off they go to another sale where an almost identical pair turns up and they find that, instead of being able to buy them and sell them for £350, they have to give something like £360 or £380 even to buy them under the hammer.

This is of course a fantastic state of affairs, the way these things have been appreciating in perhaps the last five years. But there was no thought of that with this particular dealer. This was just love of a nice piece of furniture and the fact he would like to live with it. Of course it appreciated considerably all the while it stood in his house and no doubt he could have got 100% profit on it quite easily. But this had no attraction for him. The money didn't matter. He was still content, as he said, to come down every morning and raise his hat to this piece of furniture.

Development and design of English furniture

So far I've given you the background to my life and my work. Now I want to give you some of the background to the English furniture I love, and how the need for it arose and how it came to be made.

Let's think back nearly four centuries to the end of Elizabeth I's reign. Let's imagine it's 1600, when there were only four basic pieces of furniture. There were beds, and tables, and forms, and chests. The chests were no more than boxes, thick front and ends, back and top pegged together by joiners—there were no cabinet-makers then.

All this furniture was just pegged together, so you get a thick front and back on a box, if you like. We call them coffers, with a thick lid where a woman would put all her linen, and in which, if she hadn't got enough to fill it up completely, she'd have a number of long narrow boxes with no lids lying higgledy-piggledy, to keep her silks and jewellery in. The coffer was a sort of big hold-all.

And some fifty years or more go by at least, and it's much later in the Seventeenth century before someone saw the wisdom of taking one of these open-top boxes, sticking two little bits of wood in between the legs underneath the big box and sliding an open box in, and so I like to think giving birth to a drawer. This is the first sort of drawer that was made and with its coming the coffer becomes a dower-chest. I'm not sure that I'm right in these curious beliefs I have. But you sometimes see a 'Jacobean carved oak coffer' and a 'Jacobean carved oak dower-chest.' Now if I read that description I would expect to see a box raised up on legs–short, square, stumpy legs–with a hinged cover. That's the plain coffer, and I would expect the dower-chest to be very similar except underneath it would have either one long, or two short, drawers. Of course there are earlier things actually than boxes but you can't really call them pieces of furniture. For instance at Hardwick Hall you can see a trunk of a tree. It's just shaved off square, with all the middle gouged out and a hole bored through it. I'm sure it must be the oldest piece of furniture in England–a salting-trough. But it has no feet, just lies on the ground, and you'd hardly call this a piece of furniture, though it must be very early.

So much for chests, now for tables. Most old refectory tables were at least thirty foot long, because it was customary for families to eat with their staffs, and you had just a practical table to seat perhaps fifty or sixty people. Thirty foot long, that's about the usual size. The outline is all the same–a great thick, inch-and-a-half thick, rectangular top on legs, with a stretcher. It is the legs which make them so very interesting, because you can some-times get them with a leg at each corner, joined with square rails; you can get what we call six-legged tables (that means to say it has an extra leg in the centre of the long side); you can get them standing on eight, ten, twelve, fourteen, sixteen legs. And, of course, if you get a table–an Elizabethan table–say thirty foot long, standing on sixteen legs, that means to say it has eight beautiful carved bulbous supports to each side of it, a big brother of *38* (see p. 95).

The look of that table is just grand and of course this is what makes them worth so much more money. A refectory table as such really means nothing, it's just a great long big table. The difference in value is accounted for by the number of legs on which it stands. Assuming that all the legs were of the same design, then the value is determined by whether it's on four, six, eight, ten, twelve or even more legs. These long tables have very long plank tops, usually of two boards, and I'm sure that's how you got this expression–dining at someone's board.

It's not until well into the Seventeenth century, after the East India Company got cracking bringing in tea from India and China, that the family, as it were, sloped off in the afternoons. They cleared off into a little room somewhere and drank this tea, and so you got tiny little tea-tables and eventually much bigger gate-legged tables. These are two-flap tables, some of them very big, big enough to seat perhaps ten or twelve people, but this is the sort of dining-table which follows on from the Seventeenth century to the middle of the Eighteenth, because here the family now sit down together – perhaps ten or twelve in number, leaving the staff to fend for themselves. And now that the family no longer ate with their staff but went off into this smaller room, we get, I suppose, the birth of a dining-room. Meanwhile the oak refectory tables stayed in the halls.

Now, also, they tend to put their staff into livery, and so we hear about livery cupboards and livery tables. These are virtually staff dining-tables, tables for the servants' hall. These tables were of the same type as those standing in the main halls, but they were made in pine or soft fir or elm, and were knocked together by the estate carpenter. Oft-times they'd have sycamore tops which stood up better to the harsh treatment they received from cooks and maids.

And now for the forms. There were no chairs—just forms, sometimes with turned legs, solid seats, pegged together, joined together—joint stools they're called (2 and 3, pp. 42–3). They're really the first form of seat that people sat on around these enormous long tables and you get them four foot, five foot, six foot, seven foot long. When I went to Hardwick Hall some two years ago, they gave me an inventory that had been written by Bess of Hardwick. This woman had taken a book and had just listed the furniture in her house in 1601, and I myself counted a hundred and fifty stools as against nine chairs.

What chairs there were then were like Bishop's thrones, impossible sorts of things. But then I can envisage a stool having the solid seat knocked off and someone grovelling down on the floor, picking up a handful of rush, filling in the hole, stretching a bit of silk needlework across the top and so a stool with an upholstered top comes about. And then there's not much more imagination wanted to see how a straight back could be popped on this thing and you get something like a chair as we know it, and later on arms, and so one might get an armchair.

And, of course, the beds, they were absolutely fantastic – large oak beds, eight and ten feet wide, with heavy curtains or panelled sides. There is a well-known bed which has high panelled sides and a door to enter by, so that, in fact, the bed was the bedroom.

When these old beds are stripped down just to the bare sides, you'll find that some of them have holes and it might be interesting to tell you why these holes are there. Two down each side of the bed and one at the foot, so that the bed actually turned itself into a bier after a death and they placed the five big tallow candles in these special holes. Now they're just holes, they don't do anything for the bed, but often I've been asked what those holes are for and that is the answer.

Those were the four basic things from which every other bit of furniture has come about – beds, tables, forms and chests. You see, you have to bear in mind the funny state of the country. We say funny, I suppose really it was quite natural. A few big towns, no communications, you couldn't walk down the street and have a look in a shop window and see some furniture for sale. There was nobody – no designers of furniture. If you wanted a bit of furniture in those days I take it you had to go to one of these joiners with a sketch of what you wanted more-or-less in your hand, and say to him 'Now will you make this'.

So the fashions up to the beginning of the Eighteenth century in this manner came from the patrons rather than from the joiners. There were no designs for furniture, no catalogues, no books, no shops, nothing. Most of the big homes would have had their own estate joiner and this is why, of course, all the early bits of English furniture are made in the wood that grew plentifully on the estates: mostly oak, elm of course, fruit, apple and pear, laburnum and walnut. Oak lasts the best of all those, simply because the walnut and the beech and the fruit are so soft and so susceptible to worm. But good English wainscot oak has no worm. Now I know someone is sure to write and say that they've got a coffer with a few worm-holes in it. That's quite true but if they look carefully they'll see that the worm-holes are only in the sap. They cannot attack the heart of English oak – much too hard. Sometimes when the trees were cut down there were sappy streaks down the sides and these sappy streaks, being soft, are susceptible to worm – but not the oak itself.

Now you may ask how long the timber was seasoned in those days. Well, it's known that mahogany, when that came into the country in the Eighteenth century – about 1730 – matured for anything from seven to ten years. It's usually reckoned that this wood, in log form, lay in water for about seven years and then lay out on the banks or on the ground for another three. It really did mature and, of course, bog oak, this Irish bog oak, is nothing more than an oak tree which has fallen down and lain for a great number of years in a bog or on damp ground, and when it's been resurrected, perhaps after twenty or thirty years, it's just gone almost black – and, of course, it's very hard indeed.

The same sort of process as I've described was developing on the Continent – the same state of affairs with big towns and castles and no communications. But the earlier foreign furniture seems to me to be much bigger than the early English furniture of about the same date.

It's a curious thing, but these joiners all tended to go to London and they all settled in the City and there they were making things to people's requirements. You would have to produce the design of something and they would make it. Then in 1666 along comes the Great Fire, destroys everything in the centre of the city. What few models they had were completely destroyed, all their tools destroyed, all their stocks of timber destroyed, and I envisage a vacuum. I don't really know what happened after that, but you get no mention of anything much until suddenly, out of the blue, in 1695 German and Dutch cabinet-makers came from the Continent and settled in Norfolk. They were encouraged to do so by William III – William of Orange – who had come to the English throne in 1689 with his wife Mary. They brought with them not only fine craftsmanship but new ideas of style and decoration and they helped to lay the foundations of the golden age of English furniture – the Eighteenth century.

The evolution of furniture seems to develop all through the Eighteenth century with succeeding people. Now the first man who had some real idea about furniture design was a man named William Kent. He was an architect who went to Italy about 1710 and studied architecture there for ten years. He then came back to England and he designed many houses and the furniture for them. But he could not get out of his system this heavy baroque Italianate furniture. You see, he designed things that were only suitable for mansions: enormous tables, enormous chairs for very large rooms in mansions or castles. He would design the house and then would put up suggestions for the furniture, all this very heavy baroque stuff. He never got Italy out of his mind at all. Enormous mask-heads, animals–lions and tigers jumping about in the carving, tables six, seven, eight foot long. This was all very well for these great houses but, as the population increased and as building developed to some degree, you got smaller houses built around these large homes.

And so when Thomas Chippendale followed on William Kent he must have been influenced by the sort of furniture he had seen in these houses, but he tended to lighten it – make it more usable perhaps for more ordinary people. Particularly in his later life, say from 1760 or 1770, he saw that there was a great new field opening up before him. Although he too had made furniture for mansions, with most costly chairs smothered in carving, big bold cabriole legs carved all over the knees, with ball-and-claw feet, he saw that there was this untapped source of smaller houses.

People couldn't find room for these enormous things and so he began reducing his own styles and he also reduced the cost of the pieces by putting much less work into them. He took the cabriole legs away and raised his chairs on square legs, thereby saving all that cost of preparing and carving those lovely cabriole legs, still keeping all the money, as it were, to spend on the back. So you get fine Chippendale chairs with wonderful carved backs on very ordinary square chamfered legs. Now these were done not so much for the mansions but for the next house down the scale.

Chippendale in turn was followed by other cabinet-makers, some two hundred of them living in England at the time (and bear in mind we shall never know all their names) – wonderful workmen who just made this type of furniture designed by Chippendale and set out in the *Director*[1] he published. So it's all contemporary, all period, all Chippendale, although he probably never saw any of it. And they in turn modified the designs still further, and you got a wonderful chair-maker like George Hepplewhite, apprentice to Gillow's of Lancaster, coming along, writing a book – everybody wrote a book after Chippendale–in which he said in the preface that there was nothing new in his book at all, and that he'd simply taken all Chippendale's designs and lightened them.

Where there were big, solid splat backs he pierced them. Where Chippendale splats were perhaps half an inch thick he made them three-eighths of an inch thick. He reduced every single thing. Of course he took away the big massive cabriole legs, he took away the big, square chamfered legs. He reduced these legs into a little square taper leg with a little spade foot. He chamfered off the backs of splats, took off so much that if you look

[1] *The Gentleman and Cabinet-maker's Director*

at a chair sideways it looks so thin that it's sort of dancing about.

It was Robert Adam, another great man, who introduced all this sort of filigree in design into homes, and Horace Walpole, being asked to comment on this new furniture, this neo-classic stuff that was being produced, said he disliked it intensely. 'From Kent's mahogany', he said, 'we are dwindled to Adam's filagree; grandeur and simplicity are not in the fashion.'

So it goes right on through. You get Sheraton, everybody, reducing the things down. By reducing I mean making furniture lighter, and smaller, still keeping the attractive lines. By this time, say towards the end of the Eighteenth century, there were thousands of houses, all wanting furniture. George Hepplewhite, in his great desire to create lightness in a home, even took the stretchers away from the chairs. You get mahogany chairs with the thinnest of backs, looking so frail on the thinnest of square taper or even little thin turned legs—and with no under-stretchers at all. No strength underneath and yet they're so beautifully made, they never move, they'll hold the heaviest man.

But this was the big change that took place right through the Eighteenth century: the swing of the pendulum, if you like, from the heavy William Kent furniture in the second twenty years of the Eighteenth century right through to 1800 and then, of course, if the pendulum swings one way, it swings back and, my word, doesn't it swing back into the massive Victorian furniture that was made in the middle of the Nineteenth century. The more wood that people could get into a chair or a cabinet, the heavier it became, this seemed to be the one thing that made it into a fine piece of furniture.

What I've been telling you is really in the nature of a general introduction to give you a background to the more detailed and illustrated descriptions I shall be giving you. You must bear with me if I repeat myself. I shall often do so of a purpose when I want important points to stick in your mind. Besides I know that you will need all the gen to be in handy form to help you in your viewing at sales and such-like, and to this end I shall try to give you some helpful appendices for quick reference. But before we go on to discussing pieces in detail let me first give you a few pointers to identifying and assessing old pieces.

Just how 'right' is it?

The problem of identifying old pieces from reproduction pieces rests, to my mind, mainly on the question of staining. Because, you see, if a man sets out to make an old table today he can only buy oak that is practically white. He can make his table and then he has, by some means or other, to simulate age and he can only simulate age by stain. He can knock it about with a hammer, he can use a spoke-shave on it for shaving off the rails and making them look as though they were worn. But no matter what else he does he must stain it all dark and it is the staining that gives it away.

So whenever I look, I look underneath – never at any of the parts that show. Get underneath, strike a match and have a look at the squares of the legs and under the top and I think you'll find on all old tables there will be no stain whatever, just raw wood gone dark, gone dirty. Gone a bit darker by the age they've been about, gone a bit dirty looking and greasy by virtue of the fact that the rails themselves, on the outside, would have been polished and the waxy rag would have gone underneath and so given that rail a little bit of shine, but if you look at it intently you will see *no stain*. And this applies to almost any piece of furniture under the sun.

You see, at the time these pieces were made there was no question of them being made to look old – they were just newly made. You go and have a look at any modern table you buy today. It's not stained underneath, neither were these. They were left brand-new. The attractiveness of a Chippendale chair in say 1750 was that it was brand-new. Come away, says Chippendale, from this oak and walnut. These are my new chairs in this

37

lovely new wood, this mahogany which is coming into the country now, buy these brand-new chairs. He wouldn't have sold them if he'd made them look old and knocked about. So *no stain*.

I should know, by the look of the wood, if I saw an oak refectory table that was made in mid-Victorian times. This is a queer thing to say, and I can never explain it to anybody, but in point of fact the wood itself is different. You can tell Victorian walnut from Queen Anne walnut and they're as unlike one another as I don't know what. But of course, it seems to me people make a great mistake when they set out deliberately to make a copy–they exaggerate so much the wear and tear. Of course there's wear and tear in a table that's been about for say two or three hundred years, but whenever you see, say, five-inch thick square rails running round a table, which are absolutely scooped out to such a degree that they're nearly half-round, they have just been scooped out by an over-zealous workman with a spoke-shave. Whenever you see it to that degree you can rest assured that table's wrong, or at least those rails are wrong.

Now they also have a habit of making marks and indentations to re-present the normal rough usage of these tables, because they were roughly used there's no doubt. These marks are effected by the pane of a hammer, the little half-round pointed end of the hammer which is knocked about all over the surface of the table, producing exactly the same wear marks on an 'Elizabethan' refectory table, a 'Queen Anne' walnut card table or the back of a 'Chippendale' chair. It's always the same, it's so easily recognisable.

You can often date a gate-leg table by the nature of the turning of the leg–the baluster it's called. You get one with a lovely spiral, sometimes called a barley-sugar twist; this, of course, is associated with Charles II. Then you can get them again with pretty little shaped donkey feet. This again is Seventeenth century and I suppose the very first type of gate-leg made would be the one where the gate was hinged from the very centre of the table. This is a peculiar sort of a gate-leg but it's early and, you know, the more common one has the gate hinged about three-quarters of the way along each side, but the hinges or pins on which it opens are at opposite ends of the table. So when the gates are opened one opens one way, one the other way. That's the usual form.

But a much better form if you find it is the double gate. They're just what they're called–two small gates pinned to each end of the table so that they rotate and open to an angle of about forty-five degrees both ways on both sides of the table. These double gate-legs are rare. They tend to be on larger tables—an extra support given during the Seventeenth century when they were big, possibly because families were as many as fourteen or so. They are bigger but also very pretty and you sometimes get them turned in yew. This is a lovely wood and it makes them more attractive and sought after. Again you get the prettiness of the baluster, and there's another feature which is rather nice. Instead of having just square stretchers, occasionally—usually on the better tables—the stretchers are turned to match the pattern of the baluster leg, so that you get a very 'busy' table underneath, with pretty turned legs and very pretty turned stretchers. And usually in double gate-legs the whole lot's turned—legs, double-gates and stretchers—making it so terribly lively underneath; it really is a nice table.

The yew tree, of course, has been used all through the ages. Early kitchen wheel-back chairs—those chairs, you know, with the ordinary sticks and a pierced wheel-back splat—they are always much nicer when they are made in yew (*18*, p. 63). Occasionally there are some sappy streaks which are always yellow, and which to my mind add to the attractiveness of it. It's a wood which is greatly admired and eagerly sought for. You can find tiny gate-leg tables of very early date made in yew—tops, legs, the lot—and of course these wheel-back chairs, the better type with the crinoline under-stretchers, and even early Gothic ones with the sort of church-window splats. When they're in yew they are most desirable and bring a great deal of money whenever they do turn up. They are quite rare.

You remember the suggestions I've often made on *Going for a Song* regarding identifying old chairs? The selfsame thing applies really to chests-of-drawers, cabinets, bureaux, anything with drawers in it. If you pull out the drawers—pull them completely out—the linings you'll find will be absolutely unstained. They may be a nice wainscot oak, they may be pine, but they'll nearly always be oak. But the oak will just be a mellow colour, completely unstained. These things when they were made were not made as old pieces of furniture. Their attractiveness was because they were illustrated in a catalogue published by a man who said, 'I'm prepared to make these for you'. They were in fact brand-new. And this is always a good thing to do, to look everywhere and find the absence of stain. This leads one at once to imagine such a thing be period.

39

Of course you can look for a bit of wear on the drawer-runners. In the Eighteenth century the drawers were differently made to those of earlier times. No longer were side-runners used (though you still got them for the sliding trays in wardrobes), but the base of the drawer was built up on a piece of wood called a runner on which the drawer slides in and out. There is a curious thing with drawers that's perhaps worth mentioning. It's not absolutely 100% true, but it is a bit of a guide. In nearly every piece of furniture that contained drawers and was made before about 1730 you'll find that the bottom board of the drawers has the grain running from front to back. But bear in mind I do say it is not 100% true. Then when mahogany came in and was the principal wood used, it seems the construction of drawers began to change. The cabinet-makers put the bottom boards on with the grain running across. And so from 1730 to about 1800 you get just plain drawers with the grain running across on the bottom board.

Early in the Nineteenth century another thing happens. Still the grain runs across the drawer, but inside the drawer down the long sides between the side and the bottom you'll see a tiny half-round bead, called a dust-bead. And this dust-bead was used from about 1800 onwards for some thirty years. Although the drawer-runners changed, the method of construction didn't change very much, in so far as the drawer sides were still dovetailed into the front. In the latter part of the Seventeenth century these dovetails were very, very crudely cut. They were big and crude and coarse and, coming into the Eighteenth century, the early Queen Anne and way on through, they gradually became thinner until the end of the Eighteenth century when you can find drawers similarly made, dovetails fixing the sides into the front, but the sides of the drawers no wider than an eighth of an inch thick, and beautifully dovetailed. They remain supremely strong to this very day, because here was a cabinet-maker exercising his art. No plastic wood to hide the bad fits, nothing like that. If he cut a drawer side and, when he'd pushed it into the carcase, it didn't just go in perfectly, he would cut a new side. If one looks at the drawer sides in this way you can sort of judge the age of a piece somewhat. And of course these sides themselves became much thinner, as I said, down even to the thickness of an eighth of an inch. But the drawer sides of early chests-of-drawers made between 1660 and 1700 are probably up to half an inch thick.

Chairs

Chairs are basically all of the same outline. They've all got a back, they all have a seat and invariably they all stand on four legs. It's only the shape of the legs or the shape of the back which allows one to determine the designer, the period, everything about them – by the way the legs go in or out or are turned, or the back is stuffed or has upright splats or has splats running horizontally. Every bit of detail, no matter where it occurs on a chair, tends to date it, to bring it back into the design of certain English cabinet-makers.

In the Sixteenth century there were virtually no chairs at all. Around those long refectory tables (*38–40*, pp. 95 and 96), there stood stools, stools for individuals, stools for a couple or three people—benches if you like – sometimes four foot long, six foot long, seven foot long, stretching one after the other both sides of the long, thirty-foot tables. You'll bear in mind there were no cabinet-makers, only joiners, and these stools were called 'joint' stools. They might better, perhaps, have been called 'joined' stools because they were literally joined together, pegged together. They morticed the stretchers and the framework of the stool together and then they just bored a hole through the tongue of the mortice and through the leg of the chair and held them together with a pin. Plate *2* is a good example.

The first type of joint school, and to my mind the best type, is that shown in *3*. Here you see an Elizabethan type of stool on carved turned

2 Joint stool, *c.*1670

legs, and notice the legs are not only turned but they are carved with vertical flutes and have little carved capitals at the top, and you'll see that the top-rail is also handsomely carved. In later joint stools of the Charles II period, the legs are turned and the top framework of the stool is flat. This, as you can see, is half round, carved with extremely bold gadroons–the gadroons that one associates with large refectory tables (*39*, p. 96). The majority are of course made in oak, but this is in walnut, and is a nice example.

Then one day I can see, in my queer reasoning, the solid top to a stool– because they were all solid tops–getting shaky and falling off, and I can see someone stuffing the recess inside with rushes off the floor and then stretching a piece of nice hand-needlework across the top. And so, in this way, someone gave birth to a stool with an upholstered top. At that time every large house would employ a professional embroiderer, whose job was to instruct the lady of the house and all the female staff in the use of needlework. There would be masses of needlework – Elizabethan, early needlework – practically none of it left now, but at this time there was masses of it.

And now it doesn't need much more imagination to think how someone would have fixed a back, some sort of a piece of wood or the panel from a coffer, behind this stuffed seat – an upright, slanting piece of wood which briefly gives one an outline of an early oak chair. And how later on again someone has come along and popped arms on it and virtually made some sort of thing which closely resembles an armchair as we know it today. In early times, of course, the first chairs nearly all had solid seats and solid backs, panelled and sometimes carved, sometimes inlaid with holly and bog oak in a sort of arabesque or floral design.

And of course they nearly all had turned legs united by square stretchers. This briefly is an early Seventeenth-century armchair, and single chairs were somewhat similar. This type of armchair was made all over

3 Elizabethan joint stool, c.1590

4 Charles II Yorkshire chair, c.1665

5 Charles II Derbyshire chair, *c*.1665

England but there are two peculiar types of chairs of this period that are associated with counties. *4* shows one such chair. You notice here the same idea, just some ordinary, simple, ball-turned legs with the square stretchers pegged together—you can clearly see the wooden pins holding that seat-frame together. But the back is the thing. These two rails—very wide, new arch shaping, carved, arched, arcaded. This is typical of Yorkshire. These are known and recognised as Yorkshire chairs. You see on the uprights of the back of the chair a piece of turnery—two pieces actually, one each side. These are called split balusters. They're actually two pieces of wood, stuck together and then put into a lathe and turned in that fashion, and then with a hot knife split through the joints, to make this split baluster.

The other type of chair associated with a county is illustrated in *5*. This is what is known as a Derbyshire chair. And here again you have the same idea, the plain baluster legs joined by these square stretchers, and the

same balusters on the backs of the uprights of the chair. But here, instead of having two arcaded splats running horizontally, you have a sort of perpendicular architectural design and upturned spindles with arched tops. Both the Yorkshire and Derbyshire types date from the early part of the Seventeenth century.

Now one comes along another fifty years to the reign of Charles II where we meet for the first time the introduction of cane into this country. You get the solid panelled back now giving way to either one or two cane panels, and certainly a cane seat on which would probably rest a cushion (6). These chairs were normally made in walnut. They usually have spiral underframing, the sort of thing which one is apt to call barley-sugar twists, and one usually finds the design of the turning of the legs, be they turned legs or spiral, repeated in the uprights to the back of the chair.

There's a curious thing about this type of chair – these Charles chairs as I call them (Charles II to be exact) which are always referred to as 'high-back' chairs – structurally they're terribly weak. If you look at the illustration you can imagine how easy it would be for a big or a heavy man to sit on that chair and snap the back clean off, because there are only those two tiny little uprights at the back of the cane seat. Just those two little squares of wood – nothing else – and a great high back, giving enormous leverage, and invariably one finds these backs have been broken off or are very, very weak. This perhaps is one of the reasons why these chairs are not particularly popular.

Most of them have rectangular cane panels. The pair illustrated (6) have little twin cane panels – but oft-times there's just one field of cane in the middle of the back. These chairs bring a higher price when the cane panel at the back is oval, which is more unusual. Invariably with these Charles chairs there is pierced carving of a crown of some sort in the centre of the top-rail, with two cherub supporters, one to either side, and always the carving on the top-rail is repeated below on the front stretcher.

This type of motif, particularly the cherub, carries one back to the middle of the Seventeenth century, where you commonly see on early upright wall-mirrors a sort of architectural cornice, in the centre of which there's sure to be a cherub or a cherub mask. Then take clock spandrels – those are the brass quadrants or corner-pieces on the faces of the Seventeenth-century clocks – invariably in this century they're pierced and chased and have this cherub motif engraved on them. Whenever I see these cherubs I immediately begin to think of Charles II. Of course I mustn't get too emphatic about it, because you'll recall that on French Eighteenth-century pieces of furniture one gets female busts, called caryatids, in the ormolu mounts of most French tables. They're in metal, of course, and should not be confused with the cherubs which are carved in wood on most Carolean furniture.

You'll also notice around the cane-work in the back of the chair (6) there is this carving of a leaf-scroll and a flower-head which is always referred to as a Tudor rose. You get this repeated in the centre panels of coffers and chests and dower-chests. It keeps popping up on all sorts of things and invariably these chairs are carved with this sort of flower-head and some sort of foliage.

47

7 Queen Anne wing chair, c.1710

But it's not this type of chair or the earlier ones which really interest me. The ones which I particularly like are practically all in the Eighteenth century. Here, in the early part of the Eighteenth century – and perhaps for the moment we could just talk about the first twenty years – nearly always the wood used was walnut, and it's the first inkling we get of any major use of a cabriole leg. You will see a clear example of this cabriole leg in 7. There's nothing special about that chair. It is completely stuffed all over. It certainly has wing-shaped sides, not particularly good. It has nasty, stumpy, straight back legs. It's in this cabriole leg that so much detail of style occurs and one can differentiate between the slight changes over just a few years of this period.

For example, that is a wing chair, and a true description of that would be that it stands on plain cabriole legs with a pointed toe, and with carved scroll brackets. The date of this chair is about 1710. Now it could be 15 years earlier if the cabriole leg had a decided break half-way down. I mean if, instead of it going in that sweet flowing curve, there was a

decided kink in it, or it stopped and there was a tiny moulding and then the leg went on again, this would most certainly be William and Mary. You can get this cabriole leg of square form, not rounded as is this one, but really square, tapering down to the same outline, and that also would be perhaps a few years earlier than this chair. You get a pad foot which is an ordinary round – sometimes called club-foot. You get them, as in this chair, with a pointed toe. You get them also where they're raised on hoof feet. They're very pretty. They resemble donkeys' hooves and it's a well-known characteristic to look for on all chairs from, say, about 1695 to 1720. They're all round the Queen Anne period.

If you were to compare the leg of the stool in figure 8, although it is of the same form as the chair (7), the same cabriole with those rather pretty C scrolls underneath the knee, the stool clearly shows a round pad foot as against the chair with the pointed toe. And you see 9, now that's a nice simple Queen Anne walnut stool. Just a little shaped frieze on the same legs.

By comparison, 10 is another walnut stool, practically a similar outline to 9 in walnut, but to my mind a little better, because of the extra work entailed in the carving all down the leg of the stool, deep, crisp carving which adds considerably to the value of this stool compared with the other.

50

One point I fear I've not made clear is that stools and chairs of the same period are practically matched. The early joint stools and chairs have the same bobbin-turn, or barley-sugar twist, legs.

A bit later you get William and Mary stools just the same in outline as the chairs of that period. You see *8* and *9* show exactly the same Queen Anne leg, and this leg was greatly used during this time. It was always worked out of the solid, and bear in mind that a cabriole leg was not turned in the lathe. Quite obviously today you can get a 3-inch square of wood and with a bow-saw or a band-saw cut out that shape, but everything then had to be done by the cabinet-maker on the bench, reducing the leg down and down and down, until he'd made what he considered to be a cabriole leg of a nice shape.

Then he started off to make another one exactly matching it. I've watched my father making cabriole legs even with the aid of calipers so

9 (opposite) and 10 Queen Anne stools, *c.*1710

that – say three inches off the ground – the leg would just pass through the width of the caliper. The second leg he was making had to match exactly and so a little more spoke-shave, a little more filing, a little more sand-papering, until the legs were similar. Just imagine a cabinet-maker making twelve such chairs – twenty-four times he would have to make the same cabriole leg.

And you'll notice also all the chairs for the next 20 or 30 years have rather the emphasis on strength. For instance, it would be incorrect to say that George II chairs of William Kent design were delicate. This first part of the Eighteenth century, of course, is called the baroque period, when the style was generally heavy and furniture was designed for large country seats – for mansions, not for small houses.

A wonderful example of this baroque style is to be seen in that very fine mansion, Chatsworth, which was almost completely furnished by William Kent (1686–1748). This fellow William Kent went to Italy in 1710, studied there for nearly ten years, and when he came back to England never got this heavy, mask-head, foreign sort of influence out of his system. He virtually designed everything on these lines for this type of house, and he created extremely fine furniture from the workmanship point of view, but on the other hand, unless you're in a mansion, it's completely impossible to live with. We have to wait until further into the Eighteenth century before these splats get pierced, before Thomas Chippendale alters the heavy outline, to be changed and lightened further by George Hepple-white, Robert Adam and Thomas Sheraton.

Now let's look at what is called a two-chair-back settee (11). Not a particularly fine piece of furniture because it is obviously very stiff – two rather stiff solid upright splats in what is virtually two chairs joined together, and I say solid advisedly because each splat is one piece of walnut. Then you get the solid shaped arms, known as crook arms. And still we see the cabriole leg with the pad foot.

But if this were a super settee, one would find these splats veneered, in a curly wood or a nice figured wood. It's always a sign of better quality when walnut veneer is used rather than when the splat is solid. You can just see enough round the front seat frame to see that it's veneered but the splats are solid; if they had been veneered, so many people would have noticed this, and it would have made the settee a more desirable item.

11 Queen Anne two-chair-back settee, *c.*1710

There's little doubt in my mind that all walnut chairs would carry at least double their value if they were in fact veneered on walnut or oak. It's a sign of much better quality and much better craftsmanship.

You see the settee has a loose trap seat, held by the shaped front, and covered in Queen Anne needlework. Coarse, rather, this gros-point needlework, which was virtually the only chair covering used at this time.

Now let's just compare in more detail the two Queen Anne settees—*12* and *11*. The one is so much better than the other—and we can clearly see

12 Queen Anne two-chair-back settee, c.1710

why. You see in *11* that the thing is stiff, the uprights have no shape, they're just rounded and straight up; whereas in *12* they're beautifully curved to give a much better line, they flow on into the top-rail. Again the splats on *12* resemble to some degree those on *11*, but they're not just upright splats, they're what we call spoon-back splats – shaped to make a person's back fit against them that much better.

And the outline of those two settees is just that little bit different. You see on *11* just a rather stiff start to the shepherd's crook arm, whereas the one on *12* differs in that the arms are very definitely shaped and turn down in a big scroll, and there's a little C scroll where the tops of the splats meet the top-rail. The legs are also much superior on the better settee. You see the outline, just a cabriole leg with plain corner-brackets – that's exactly the same in each, but to my mind *12* has definitely the better-shaped knee, and it's carved with a nice closed shell and a bluebell drop. And finally compare the stretchers – in the poorer settee turned stretchers, in the better settee turned stretchers running from front to back, but a shaped, moulded stretcher uniting them. Now if you can recognise points like this, you can see why *12* would make probably twice as much as *11*.

13 shows a chair which to my mind is particularly interesting, because oft-times such a chair is referred to as a cockfighting chair. One can see how this idea comes about, because you have the seat, as it were, the wrong way round. In other words, you sit with your back facing to the front, with no supports. You sit astride this chair, resting your arms on the top of the shaped, flat upholstered arms, and this is why the chair tapers off at the back to such a very narrow part. The idea of sitting this way round and giving the illusion of, say, a judge watching a cockfight, is emphasised even more, because at the back of this chair there is an adjust-

13 George I library armchair, *c.1720*

able flap which works up on a ratchet, and so one could readily have a table on which one could write. In the backs of these stubby arms there are also some fittings – a hinged fold-back drawer which would take pens, pencil, inkpots and the like. You see, it was thought a man would sit there and record the progress of a cockfighting match. You notice there is a small drawer in the seat frame, which was obviously for paper. This chair we are looking at is about 1720, in walnut, with a plain cabriole leg and the pad foot and a rather pretty, turned under-stretcher. But, although it's quite an early chair, the cockfighting theory has been completely disproved. It's nothing more nor less than a library armchair.

This was a working chair for a gentleman, who might be studying. He sat as I've described, the wrong way round so to speak, put up the adjustable flap, and could have all he needed to hand, pens and inks and everything, and even a little supply of paper in the drawer, so that he had virtually, if you like, a very early Eighteenth-century office chair. They were made later in mahogany, and some were country-made in oak. But that's a very good chair and a nice example of what brass nails do, and how they emphasise the line on leather.

As a matter of fact this chair was shown on the television programme *Going for a Song* and caused quite a lot of comment. Many people wrote in disagreeing that it was a library chair, and insisting that it was, in fact, a cockfighting chair. But all reference books, and particularly the *Dictionary of English Furniture*,[1] definitely come out in favour of a library chair, and I think the very quality of the workmanship and of the wood used shows that these chairs were intended for libraries, rather than for fighting-cock pits. As a matter of fact this chair is of particular interest because it belonged once to the poet, John Gay (1685–1732). Clearly he must have used it for writing, for a poem in manuscript was subsequently found in the drawer.

It is a remarkable thing how little details of style and period are often repeated on different pieces of furniture, pieces that have quite separate uses. Yet if they are of the same period, these little things always seem to tie up. For example in *14* the one thing that attracts me most to this chair, or the one little point to notice, is the hair-claw foot. This makes the chair George II, but curiously enough, if it is compared with the swan-neck

[1] *The Dictionary of English Furniture* by Ralph Edwards (2nd edition, London, 1954).

14 George II Gainsborough armchair, c.1735

15 Pair of Chippendale armchairs, c.1760

cornice of the bureau-bookcase (see p. 163), you'll see that the latter has two large gilt flower-heads on the top of the swan-neck cornice and, if you look at the chair arms, there is another example of those flower-heads. These little details, if one can remember them, do so help to identify the age or date of a piece of furniture. Another example is the comparison between the heavy gadrooning on the Elizabethan refectory table (39) and exactly the same type of gadrooning found on the Elizabethan joint stool (3).

Now, here I've shown a pair of armchairs (15). You'll notice principally that the splats, whilst they're still upright, are pierced. This is an early type of Chippendale chair. Notice how the cabriole leg has given way to a square leg, which has the inside edge of the square shaved off. In fact this is known as a chamfered leg. This is an ordinary type of chair that shows the change-over from the William Kent-ish, rather solid period, for which I have only qualified regard.

The furniture is being designed now by a man named Thomas Chippendale (1718–1779). This man obviously sees that there is a market opening up to him other than the extremely fine mansions in the country. There is a middle class appearing in England, who cannot give the money required to buy superb, wonderful chairs. So here you have an example of a pair of chairs in which he's cut the detail and the cost of the cabinet-making down to the barest minimum. He's got a pierced splat, which is usual with Chippendale chairs, no carving, a little, shaped top-rail, again no carving, though sometimes these cresting-rails as they're called are profusely carved. The arms have a little bit of shape but are quite simple. Formerly an arm on this type of chair might have finished in an eagle's head, with an eagle's beak, and scales all up the arms–a lot of work. Then he's taken that lovely carved – but expensive – cabriole leg with the ball-and-claw foot completely away. These have got square straight stumps, joined together by square stretchers. As simple as they can be.

Chippendale of course designed superb chairs, developing his own style of cabriole from the very bold cabriole legs of the George II period, and he used it on many of his finest chairs, with ball-and-claw feet. The backs he absolutely smothered in carving, but all this, of course, cost money. You see with 16 (p. 61) a dining-chair with cabriole legs at the front, but quite plain. It has plenty of wood for the ball-and-claw at the bottom, but you notice a little bit of extra labour here on the top-rail. This is what Chippendale did. A little bit of detail on the top just to liven them up a bit, but he has left the plain cabriole leg which has just the same form, if you compare them, as the octagonal drop-leaf dining-table (46 on p. 102). This is a good type of chair. It's rather heavy, of course, but you see how nicely this type of dining-chair would fit in and sit round the table. The carved little C scroll bracket on the tops of the legs of this chair takes the same form as the scroll bracket on the table. But on the chair it is relatively plain, ending in a plain simple scroll, just to provide a nice finish to the leg.

In 1754 Thomas Chippendale issued a catalogue.[1] Now this was an extraordinary thing, because this was the first time ever that a comprehensive catalogue had been so issued. Published at $3\frac{1}{2}$ guineas, it ran to three editions, the last (with two hundred illustrations) being published in 1760. A copy of the first edition (if perfect) would fetch something over £150

[1] *The Gentleman and Cabinet-Maker's Director*

today. Here he gave a series of plates in which some of his most superb pieces of furniture appear, and at the same time he also illustrated simple pieces of furniture, all of which he said he was prepared to make. He gave cross-sections of all the mouldings, gave the dimensions of every piece of furniture, and you can quickly see how this became the very first bench-book, one might call it, ever to appear. It was taken up by at least 200 extremely fine cabinet-makers of this period whose names we shall never know, but who did very, very fine work solely out of Chippendale's books. This man had more influence on furniture than any other man who has ever lived. Of course there was no copyright in those days, so that Chippendale, having sold this bench-book at three and a half guineas (which was good money then), gained no further benefit from the number of people who made furniture to his designs.

It's a curious thing how the second-hand value of these chairs remained very low indeed for some two hundred years. My father had a shop in Reading and he used to hire a flat trolley, a horse-drawn trolley, which he drove out to any one of the small villages around, shouting that he was giving £1 each for old chairs. This was in my lifetime – and he would be forced to leave that village, either because it would be impossible to put any more chairs on his trolley, or because he'd run out of money. Of course he made very little because he brought these chairs back to his shop and, if they were a bit rickety or tatty, he put them right and sold them for only 30/– each.

You know, Thomas Chippendale not only saw the new market opening up, but he brought a new dimension to chair design – in a word, comfort. He designed chairs that someone could actually relax in. The earlier type of chair was so bold and most uncomfortable, but in the second half of the Eighteenth century I suppose some of the most comfortable chairs ever produced were made. For example, this type of chair in 17 is what we call an open-arm easy and is extremely comfortable. It's got an upholstered seat and back – not a sprung seat, I hasten to add (springing in a stuffed seat didn't come in until the Nineteenth century), and it's sometimes known as a Gainsborough chair. The idea simply was that it had this wide seat – you know what a Gainsborough lady looks like in her portrait, masses of clothes – and so this chair had ample proportions to accommodate the fashion more comfortably.

17 Chippendale open-arm chair, *c.*1780

To digress for a moment, I'm sure everyone knows what a wheel-back kitchen armchair is like. A solid seat with a pierced splat cut in the shape of a wheel and with turned spindles. Absolutely all wood. *18*, which is in yew, is a good example. And yet to my mind one of the most comfortable chairs you could possibly sit in. No cushions, because these chairs were sort of built to a body. Comfort today appears to be quite a different thing to

18 Eighteenth-century wheel-back chair

what it was years ago. It seems to me comfort today means wallowing in about nine inches of foam cushions. You fall back in this mass of foam, which almost envelops you, and everyone says 'Marvellous!' and 'Isn't that lovely?' And my word, when you can get out of it and when you do get out of it, how your back aches! Now you never get an aching back in an old kitchen wheel-back chair. This chair was made to give ease to a body.

As we did with the Queen Anne settees, it's now possible to compare in detail the two chairs *17* and *19*. *19* is obviously the same type of Chippendale Gainsborough armchair. The padded arms, the upholstered seat and the raising of the chair on the square moulded legs, all just the same. The main

19 (opposite) Chippendale open-arm chair, *c*.1780

20 Chippendale armchair, *c*.1770

difference in the two chairs of course is in the turning outwards of those scroll arms and the pretty-shaped uprights that support the armrests. This again makes a great difference in the two chairs. Some people might feel they'd like 17, others would prefer 19. But these little differences in design may make big differences in value.

Now if you compare 15 and 20, you see there's a lot of similarity, except that a carver has got to work on 20. Instead of the pierced splat being quite plain, it's carved. The top-rail is literally smothered. The back uprights instead of being square are moulded, just to give it a little extra finesse. The arms are still quite shapey, not quite the self-same shape, but on the flat part of the end of the arm you can just see a round carved patera. And you notice still the same square legs and stretchers, but some-one has added these pierced corner brackets – all of which make that chair just that much better than the plain one.

You will have heard of some furniture called Chinese Chippendale. This doesn't mean that Chippendale went to China. It only means that he was influenced by Chinese design, and the introduction of this pierced corner bracket just shows the influence creeping in. 21 clearly shows this and the points I want to make. The square legs with the applied fret are rather pretty, because half way down the leg the fret stops and there are three little bluebell drops carved in the solid. Now that unusual detail makes those rather nice. The fret corner-bracket is retained and then, coming on to the back of the chair, you see the splat is interlaced – a boldish design, because this is a big chair, and up go the corners, carved with the outlines of Chippendale beaded C scrolls. There are three of them – all very shallow – that go to make the outline of the back: two lying, as it were, face upwards, and one reversed in the centre, lying face downwards. This all adds up to a chair made round about 1765, executed from his designs when he was influenced by oriental motifs.

Now regarding the Chinese influence on this chair I think perhaps this pierced bracket, the fret legs and the type of back are probably the first evidence of Chippendale's mind turning a little to the Chinese. You'll recall that he did go almost the whole oriental hog and made armchairs that had wide pierced fret all over the backs and under the arms, and tiny applied fret all down the legs, and all with pierced brackets.

I think 20 also shows the nature of the carving at this period. You can

see instantly how deep, how crisp the carving is on that top-rail. This is another thing to look for. I always look deeply into the carving on any chair, and you see where there are acanthus scrolls over the front of that cresting-rail, well, the background of the rail is as clean as any other part of the chair where there is no carving at all. I know that that part of the chair has been reduced down and a man has paid so much attention to the background that it looks just as though there is a plain, polished rail that has had a bit of leaf carving applied to it, rather than a piece of wood with the leaves carved out of the solid in high relief. The carving is always so crisp and nice and of course that can only be easily done on that fine, hard Cuban mahogany. When you get into soft Honduras it's very difficult to make the carving so crisp.

It's a curious thing, you know, how little has ever been written trying to tell people clearly what to look for in deciding whether a chair is old or new. You see, there are many reference books that give the outlines of backs of chairs. You can find these illustrated and so, when you look at a chair, by reference to the book you can say, 'This is a Chippendale chair, this is a Sheraton chair, this is probably Hepplewhite'. But it seems to me that no one is willing even to try to put down in black and white certain guides as to how one can determine whether this Chippendale-type chair, the back of which conforms to an illustration in a book, is of the period – that is, say, made in 1770 – or whether it was in fact made in 1960.

And yet to me it does not seem so very difficult. It is largely a question of eyesight. It's necessary to tip the chair completely upside down and examine underneath the stretcher-rails and underneath and inside the seat-rails. So get the chair upside down, look at all those four seat-rails and underneath the stretchers. They should have no stain on them at all. They will perhaps be dirty-looking where someone has lifted a chair from here to there over a period of years; there will be perhaps greasy or shiny marks underneath the seat-rail; but there will be virtually no stain. For one point which is often missed is so simple, namely that when a period chair was made, that chair was sold to people as a brand new chair. There was no question of Chippendale supplying people with old chairs. George Hepplewhite, when he made a chair, made a brand new chair and underneath the seat-rails and the stretcher-rails there would be no stain to give the appearance of age. Pick up any modern chair you might buy today anywhere; you will find underneath the rails there is no stain at all. Its attractiveness, and the attractiveness of a period Chippendale chair, is to some degree the same – that they were both new in design, and they were certainly new in manufacture, one made in, say, 1780, the other in 1965. Neither had any stain.

Then there is another little thing which helps, although it's not always there. In the centre of the back of the seat-rail, immediately under the splat when the loose seat is taken out, there is usually cut a number. This is a number cut in Roman figures by the straight half-inch pane of a chisel. The numbers were I, II, III, IV and so on. It just meant that when a cabinet-maker had laid out his wood and had decided to make, say, six single chairs and two armchairs – arms as we call them – he just marked them in this fashion. Now that numeral is not always there, but it's just nice when it is. More often than not you can pick up a chair today and see the figure 6. An arabic 6. And this of course immediately means that you are looking at something which is modern.

In addition to the unstained framing of the chair and perhaps these roman figures, another good test of period is to try and lift a chair by using only the forefinger. Put the forefinger through the pierced splat and lift it up in the air. You should be absolutely delighted to put it down again, because the wood used in the Eighteenth century was really superb Spanish mahogany. It came from Cuba and it really was a most delightful wood to use. Hard and weighty. And if you once learn the weight of an Eighteenth-century chair you will quickly know when you pick up a chair which is of late Nineteenth-century manufacture. The difference in weight is quite surprising. And I'll tell you why. In the early Nineteenth century apparently the economics of the Colonies even affected the manufacture of chairs. Because the government of the time decided that an import duty should be placed on all wood coming into the country, other than that which came from the Colonies. One of the Colonies exporting mahogany was British Honduras. And so of course the import of Cuban mahogany stopped. Cabinet-makers, because of the import duty, instead bought the softer British Honduras mahogany, much lighter in weight.

Apart from the difference in weight between an Eighteenth- and Nineteenth-century mahogany chair, do bear in mind, too, the difference in colour. Here again there are reasons. The Eighteenth-century wood

69

matured anything up to ten years before use, seven years perhaps floating in log form and three years lying drying out. Now this really made for a wonderfully mature sort of colour in this mahogany. In the Nineteenth century, however, it's much lighter in colour, as well as weight.

Another thing which oft-times people overlook is the fact that on a period chair no amount of polishing or cleaning can rub up white edges. This is a thing which is often seen and not recognised as being a sign of a much more modern chair. It means that the chair has been stained to give it some sort of simulation of age, or of colour, to match a period piece, and an excessively keen butler or maid can, by application of furniture polish and plenty of elbow grease over a few years, rub through that stain and bring up white edges down the uprights of the legs.

So to summarise, pointers to an Eighteenth-century chair are: no stain, sometimes a Roman number cut with a straight half-inch chisel in the middle of the back frame of the chair, the weight of a chair, the colour of a chair, and no white edges. And bear in mind also about colour – on a period piece everything will appear the *same* colour. So that if you see dark legs, dark stretchers, dark seat-rail, dark arms, and dark top-rail but a light splat, it's so simple: it just means the splat is a replacement.

So many people talk about the patina on a chair or table or anything and of course this is, in itself, highly desirable. Patina is virtually the surface appearance. It comes really by loving care, that is all. Every chair and table starts off in the same way – raw wood – polished by turps and linseed oil, and then the patina depends on the care which it receives over the next fifty or a hundred years. This can't be properly reproduced so the general appearance of a chair also has some bearing on formulating opinion as to whether it be old or new.

There's also a useful tip to help you determine whether the armchairs (or 'arms' as we call them) in a set really belong to it. A genuine armchair which is original to the set will always have a front seat-rail that is a couple of inches or so wider than the seat-rail of any of the single chairs. Oft-times single chairs have been known to be 'armed' up. If the front seat-rails of the single and armchairs are the same length then you may be sure that the arms have been added – and a lot comes off the value.

If you refer once again to *20*, this is a Gothic Chippendale chair, by reason of the Gothic windows in the back. There they are outlined by the pierced splat, which also has those rather elongated pear-drops or tears which are typical of the period. This chair is about 1770 to 1775, when you get wine-glasses on drawn stems with just such a tear as that in them. And you get nice cut-glass lustres of perhaps ten years later with lovely cut pear-shaped drops. And as I've said before you get this recurring use of motifs over and over again, particularly a bit later on in the Eighteenth century when Robert Adam's inlays of husks and laurel and honeysuckle were appearing as engraving on silver or as decoration on Wedgwood pottery. You could pretty well date a mustard pot to 1780 by seeing a little pierced border of pretty little swags of laurel, in the same manner as a table might be inlaid to the design of Robert Adam.

Now here's another ordinary type of chair, in fact a very ordinary Chippendale chair, 22. You couldn't have anything much more simple than that—a plain upright splat, not very shapey arms, reduced square legs, and reduced square stretchers. The only point about this chair, and the only reason it's mentioned, is because it's rather unusual. It's known as a campaign chair, and the whole thing folds up almost to nothing. The sides are hinged in a sort of concertina action, so that when

22 Chippendale campaign chair, c.1800

they are unhooked, they just fold absolutely flat back towards the back of the chair. These were the sort of chairs that generals took when they went off to war. Just plain ordinary mahogany, but it's interesting to think that these fellows when they went off to war took with them a few Chippendale chairs to sit on.

Now we come on to George Hepplewhite (d. 1786) and *23* shows a Hepplewhite armchair. George Hepplewhite, reputedly the finest English chair-maker, apprenticed to Gillow of Lancaster, was influenced by the French. He had a great feeling for this French cabriole leg, as you see in this interesting chair. He wrote a book, as did Chippendale, and as did everyone who followed. In the preface he said that he would take the previous designs of Chippendale and lighten them, and by lightening them he meant he would reduce them and fine them down. For example, in this photograph you see a break away from the one upright pierced splat. He has a central pierced splat composed really of two wavy spars joined together with two similar wavy spars and matching uprights.

In *24* you can see that he's gone a stage further and taken all the splats away completely. There you have virtually the same moulded outline of the back of the chair, which is just stuffed. And the cabriole leg is much thinner than the cabriole leg of Chippendale, and much, much thinner than the cabriole leg of William Kent – it's now a finely drawn leg. And so in this way Hepplewhite transforms the so solid, so firm, so rocklike furniture of the early Eighteenth century into something that begins, as it were, to dance about by comparison.

Look at that chair in *24* – absolutely alive with shape. Look at the back leg and the back support: from the top of the chair right down past where the arm joins it, past where the seat-rail is morticed into it and down to that shapely back leg. You may be surprised when I tell you that from the top to the bottom is one piece of wood. Just look at all the shapes there that dodge in and out. It goes in and out and down and round, and of course there is a well-known saying that if a man can make a chair he can make anything. And my word, I really think that's true.

Now if you look at this chair, the back supports are at different angles and you can see how the uprights, so to speak, bend about and spread all ways. It's a miracle of craftsmanship when you realise that that back upright probably comes out of a piece of wood, maybe six inches wide and

23 Hepplewhite armchair, c.1780

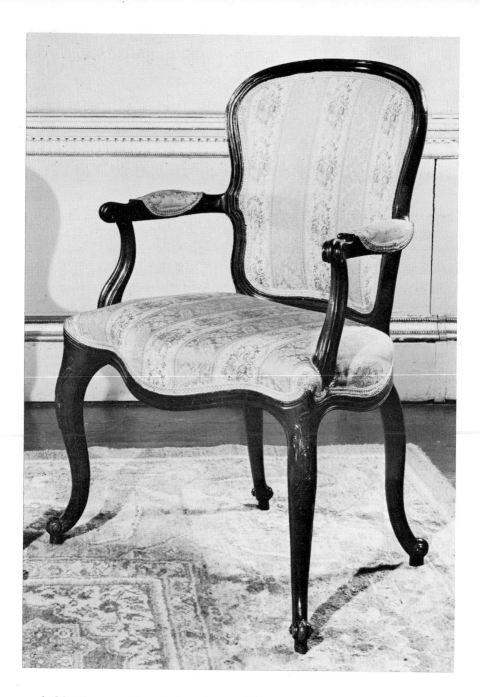

probably three or four inches deep, all cut away to get that one support with all its twistings and writhings that cunningly accommodate the square joints where the arms join on. The seat frames have to mortice exactly into another straight bit on that leg, so that the leg itself, as it were, flows out of the seat frame.

You'll notice that these chairs have four cabriole legs, the back legs also finely shaped and with C scroll toes. Now, if you compare *23* and *24* you see the back legs on *23* are rounded but are virtually straight. It's true they splay out at the foot, but in point of fact they're what we call straight-back legs. On *24* there are four nearly equal cabriole legs and this makes the chairs even more desirable. It must be remembered that the price range of chairs depends, to a great degree, on the amount of detail that one sees. The very fact that one chair stands on four cabriole legs and another has just the two front legs cabriole makes a difference in the price. Similarly the fact that a card-table has two carved cabriole front legs and the square back legs makes a big difference in the price. It's all a question of comparison.

Now you see this heart-shaped chair (*25*). Here is George Hepplewhite designing chairs with differently shaped backs. This heart-shaped back is always Hepplewhite. He was the man who introduced this particular pattern to the backs of chairs, and also the Prince of Wales plumes. You see them carved there in the top of the central splat (*26*). But the point about this chair, if you compare it with a Chippendale chair, is what he's done to all the wood. Compare it with *16* (p. 61) and you will see how much wood Hepplewhite has taken away from a heavy splat like that. Look how he has reduced the splats of the middle uprights, and you see the skill of the carver there in tying that knot of ribbon (*26*). Look how a clever man just puts a few little kinks, as it were, in the mahogany and turns wood into ribbon. And look at the swags of drapery there. So light that they really look like material. And again the arms, look at this little shaped arm here, carved with bluebell drops or husks (*27*). The result has been to reduce the arm from being a massive, heavy support into a slim graceful shape.

And there's a thin square taper leg, moulded, a bit of carving down it and all the stretchers taken away. Yet this chair is as firm as a rock. Although the wood itself is reduced to a bare minimum, the art of this cabinet-maker is in the strength of the chairs that he produced. They stand as firm today as when they were made nearly two hundred years ago. As firm, but so greatly fined down because of his desire for extra lightness and prettiness. It might seem difficult to some people to realise how strongly these chairs are made, because after all, the stretchers that he has taken away are no more than strengthening bars that hold all the legs together. And yet chairs made by George Hepplewhite and his con-

25 (opposite) and 26 Hepplewhite armchair, c.1785

temporaries in the loveliest of fine Spanish mahogany are as firm and as strong as any. It's absolute sheer English cabinet-maker's supreme workmanship at its Eighteenth-century best.

Always assuming the articles to be old, the value depends on the extra detail, the extra workmanship, the finer quality. It's a curious thing that the value of an article is not always dependent on its age.   For example, if one recalls the Charles chairs that we discussed earlier, they are nothing like so valuable as Chippendale chairs. On the other hand, a rare type of Hepplewhite chair is worth appreciably more than a good Chippendale chair. This is taste or fashion, or something, but invariably, where you

77

27 Detail of 25

have equal types of chairs designed by the same cabinet-maker, their value varies according to the extra detail.

And of course some chairs for some reason are much scarcer than others. Why this should be I don't know, but take for instance *28* which is an ordinary tub chair, a tub-shaped chair. It seems to me this is something of an adaptation of an upholstered wing chair, but these chairs are scarce. This type of easy chair, with its leather upholstery, stood about in libraries and they're nothing like so common as dining-chairs. This, in itself, makes it worth much more money than, say, a Chippendale armchair.

All these Hepplewhite chairs are round about 1780, but you still see the French influence. This chair is very much Anglicised but, although everything else has gone absolutely English, those little bits of leather-covered pads on the arms are retained from the Hepplewhite chair (24).

28 is a rare chair. Again no stretchers you see, and yet absolutely firm. And what I like is that it shows wood all the way round. The correct catalogue description for this chair would be 'a Hepplewhite armchair within a moulded show-wood frame'. Now occasionally these chairs are stuffed all over, but then you tend to lose the line which is dependent on the upholsterer's art. Here then is a chair with a show-wood frame and it would bring more money than one that has no visible outer wood frame.

These library chairs were invariably upholstered in leather and you see this one is nailed all the way round: every edge has brass nails which show up the shape and the style and the line. Of course leather is not liked these days but a few years ago everything was in leather – Chesterfield suites, upholstered seats on dining-chairs, and so on. But with fashions changing and women's clothes becoming thinner and thinner, I might say I've seen many ladies sit down to dinner at night and absolutely shudder, because they've sat on stone-cold leather.

Another thing which is a little bit awkward for women is the old-fashioned horse-hair seat one finds often on dining-chairs – they're very prickly through thin clothes. Of course there was no central heating in the Eighteenth century. Our ancestors were probably more hardy, not so pampered as we are, and would need and did wear many more clothes, so that they wouldn't feel these things as we do today.

You will recall how we've said that George Hepplewhite tended to lighten everything – the library chair (28) is, of course, a big bold chair for a man to sit in at his ease with a book. These tub chairs are wonderfully comfortable and need to be strong, and so are perhaps a little heavier, but there's still this restraining influence to make it lighter and lighter. Now compare the leg of 28 with the leg of 20. You see, it has become tapered, shaved and thinned down, and now it's reeded, as it's called, with those vertical flutes, again with the idea of making it a little bit more decorative.

29 shows a very ordinary dining-chair. See how these legs have been thinned and how the splat has been reduced, no longer a big wide pierced

central splat but three little upright spars in that square-shaped back—
nothing more. The legs tapered, thinned right down—and no stretchers.
This picture shows it well.

It oft-times puzzles people to differentiate between Hepplewhite and

Sheraton designs – especially in dining-chairs. So let's look at some shield-backs, a well-known and lovely form of late Eighteenth-century dining-chair. If one were asked to distinguish between, say, a set of Hepplewhite and a set of Sheraton shield-back dining-chairs, the very fact that some have stretchers would lead me to say that they are Sheraton. A chair with exactly the same back but no stretchers would, to my way of thinking, be Hepplewhite. However, it mustn't be imagined that all shield-back chairs must be Sheraton if they have stretchers. Comparison is rather the other way round. A shield-backed chair without stretchers would definitely be Hepplewhite, but there are many Hepplewhite chairs which still retain the cross-stretchers, such as 30.

You see 31 shows a shield-back Sheraton dining-chair. It is the usual form of chair of this nature – moulded framework, a pierced upright splat, upholstered seats, square legs and stretchers. This is a simple type of shield-back chair, but you can get far better ones. 32 is a Hepplewhite armchair. Here you have roughly the same outline in the back – a moulded shield-shape and five shaped spars, as it were radiating from a little half-moon at the base of the shield and carved with acanthus leading on to the top camel-hump part of the shield. Now, that's a pretty back and it stands on square, fluted tapered legs.

You notice the use of the word 'fluted'. Here again a little more work. 31 just has plain, square taper legs. These in 32 are square taper legs, but fluted, which is just that much better. And they also have what we call spade feet. That makes more work again and, of course, it becomes a better chair. But the feature of this armchair 32 is in the so delicately-shaped arms. Just look at those arms, how they rise up, twist about all ways, and just turn that fairly good chair into a very good armchair.

And then again in 30 – a Hepplewhite single chair – just the same outline as 31, a moulded shield-shaped back, but look at that splat. As I've said, George Hepplewhite was the first man to use Prince of Wales plumes. You see them carved there on the top of the chair – you see them hung with all that drapery and the carved rosettes. That's not material, but it hangs so beautifully that you might think so. In fact that's carved wood, and if you see a chair with a back like that on it, of course you say at once 'What a beautiful back!'

There again the legs are similar but they are moulded – they're a little bit

31 Sheraton shield-back chair, c.1790

32 Hepplewhite shield-back armchair, c.1785

better than the ordinary straight tapered legs, but perhaps not quite so good as the chair legs of *32*. But the back of *30* is absolutely superb. Hepplewhite was bent on reducing, reducing, reducing, fining things down and making chairs come completely alive. This man Hepplewhite as a designer and maker of chairs is without doubt my favourite. There's no question about this chair-maker. He produced some chairs whose outlines, to my mind, are absolutely unsurpassed by anybody.

Now one comes along to the turn of the century and just about then– round about 1800 – we find this type of chair (*33*). Now here again is this Hepplewhite and these are light in design, and also very light in weight, because these are what we call painted and decorated Hepplewhite chairs. They're made in beech and you can see that all the decoration has worn off the arms which show the yellowish colour of beechwood. This type in its original decoration can be extremely pretty. Ebonised in some cases as these were, just picked out with some white lines and possibly gold rings around the legs and the arms, but always great care taken with the decoration. For instance, take the white line running round the arm. If it starts off just a quarter of an inch from the edge, so it follows the line of that arm, never wavering, that same distance from the edge the whole way round.

Plate *34* shows another painted and decorated armchair, made in beech, in the French taste, probably from a design by George Hepplewhite. A nice design for the back, eight spokes, as it were, radiating from the oval central patera (Robert Adam liked this type of 'wheel-back'), a moulded framework holding the spokes with a carved blossom at the top, shaped moulded arms and an upholstered seat with moulded cabriole legs, and the usual shaped moulded apron carved in its centre with flowers and foliage. A nice type of chair, 1780–90.

But let's go on a bit to what have become extremely fashionable these days – Regency chairs (*35*). In my younger days these chairs were known to stand on what everyone called Trafalgar-shaped legs. This actually dates these chairs to about 1805. Nowadays, of course, the word Trafalgar is dropped and this chair stands on what is called the sabre-shaped leg. Whether the new description is a great improvement on the old, I don't know. Anyway now the chair is beginning to get just a little more weight in the design and I'm sure everyone can envisage this chair forty or fifty years afterwards developing into something quite ugly, quite heavy; and

33 Pair of Hepplewhite painted and decorated armchairs, c.1800

34 Hepplewhite painted and
decorated armchair, c.1790

so we get the birth of mid-Victorian furniture.

I suppose that's the swing of the pendulum right from William Kent in, say, 1725 with his heavy baroque furniture, through the various designers who kept on lightening Kent's designs, refining them, thinning them right down, so that they danced about, until, at the turn of the Nineteenth century, the designs gradually became heavier and heavier, through the Regency, through George IV and William IV and right through Victoria's reign up to the end of the century.

These chairs shown in 35 are rather unusual. A sort of rather pretty swag or shoulder line of a woman's dress for a back. They were from a long set of dining-chairs. I think there were as many as twelve and two arms in this set, and they'd be highly desirable today. You see they still have this idea of leather on the seats. This is only Morocco or grained leather, not a skin, but this old idea of leather upholstery still hangs on into the Nineteenth century; and I suppose of all things now, it's the one material not used.

I've not mentioned any designs of chairs by Robert Adam (1728–92), a very well-known architect who envisaged one harmonious whole in every room he designed. He reintroduced into chairs and into every piece of furniture he designed a neo-classical influence. All his designs derived, as it were, from classical Italy and Greece – the honeysuckle coming in, the swags, the oval patera, the rams' heads, urns, vases, all these.

Curiously enough all this tails off with his death and the introduction of Regency furniture, influenced by Nelson's victories, the Battle of the Nile and Trafalgar. These exploits were so much in the news that furniture designers turned to Egypt for their designs in the best Regency furniture and so we get things of early Egyptian art – sphinx heads and monuments – decorating the supports of chairs. The arms terminate sometimes in sphinx heads, and all this Egyptian influence came about because of the wars against Old Boney.

Of course you get the same influence in French furniture of the First Empire under Napoleon. The ormolu ornaments commemorating war and all kinds of things, all the ormolu mounts, all tied up with great national events. You see this influence not only in furniture but in porcelain and the mounts of porcelain, in minerals which were quarried and worked – like wonderful Blue John, or Derbyshire Spar – in clock sets with the two side ornaments in the form of obelisks like Cleopatra's needle.

35 Regency sabre-leg chairs, *c*.1815

There are many types of Regency hall chairs, often made especially for a family, because they do seem to carry somewhere on them painted escutcheons of arms. But occasionally you come across a hall chair something like *37*. This to my mind is most unusual. It's extremely delicate, the manner in which it's carried out: the tiny little round solid seat, a rather late Georgian type of turning on the front legs, spreading out a bit at the base, but a very pretty back. You see the introduction of the anthemion, or honeysuckle, with the acanthus, and the manner in which the sort of rather peculiar-shaped panelled back is terminated by the pair of eagles' heads. They're beautifully carved – the plumage down their necks superbly done, and the rings which are in the eagles' mouths are actually carved from the solid. Now that's what I call a pretty hall chair as against many others which, although fine quality, can't always be called pretty.

36 illustrates a painted and decorated papier-mâché chair. This style of spoon-back chair is tending to get back a bit towards Queen Anne design, but is so obviously Victorian. The nice shape of the cabriole leg – that's all but gone. And the rather stiff back legs. But the spoon-back – that's well shaped, and painted very prettily. All in papier-mâché. This is really quite fantastic work, when you consider how strong that chair is, what heat, what damp, what weight it'll stand up to. When you think that this is really nothing more than paper and pitch, you realize what a wonderful invention it was. Originally Persian, it was first used for ornaments and picture-frames, and was first patented for the manufacture of furniture by Henry Clay of Birmingham in 1772.

Clay would make an iron framework of the outlines of that chair and would then paper it. It would then be dressed with pitch and oil, raised to a terrific heat, and allowed to cool. Then when quite cold, it would be covered with another layer of paper. The same procedure, over and over and over again, until you get perhaps an inch thickness of paper, which assumes the strength of wood. It's supposed to be absolutely heat and damp resistant; it's terribly strong. It's quite fantastic to think a chair like

36 Early Victorian
papier-mâché chair, c.1855

37 Late Georgian hall chair, c.1815

this can really be made of japanned paper. This particular chair is the one that was awarded to one of the successful collectors who succeeded in winning a customer prize in *Going for a Song*. This papier-mâché work with its very individual decoration is somewhat reminiscent of early Eighteenth-century red and gold oriental lacquer work, which also has dozens of layers.

About this time, the turn of the century, you get the reintroduction of caning. If you recall this was introduced to England in the middle of the Seventeenth century when you got cane panels in the backs and seats of chairs. We now get a type of chair produced called a bergère, after a French original. It's really another big sort of library armchair with a cane seat, cane back and cane sides. Also in this Regency period we get a preference for brass as an inlay. Many of these chairs are literally smothered with brass – brass stars, brass lines, rectangular shaped panels inset in the backs of chairs in a nice diaper design, all in brass.

I must say this type of chair is very attractive because it's not big. One of the drawbacks to a good set of, say, Chippendale dining-chairs is that they are on the large side. You must remember, they were made for large dining-rooms, to sit round large dining-tables. By now people are often being forced to reduce and it seems that after every death there is a removal to a house that's not quite so large. The dining-room is smaller and it is an advantage to have small dining-chairs. Perhaps this is one of the reasons why this type of chair on the sabre-shaped leg finds itself in great demand.

All through the first thirty to forty years of the Nineteenth century one gets a miscellaneous assortment of chairs, generally on these shaped legs, oft-times on a new kind of cabriole leg. It's not truly a cabriole but a rather heavy-shaped leg, usually with a claw foot and a big lioness or lion mask on the top of the knee. This type of leg is called a monopodium. It figures on heaps of things, particularly on chairs and their supports, and on many tables. Console tables often have their one leg decorated with a rather peculiar lion mask.

This is all well into the Nineteenth century and eventually we come along to the type of chair, often in oak, which became very fashionable in Victorian times. There's no particular design worth trying to remember. That perhaps is a very bold statement but what I really imply is that these designs were so massive. Ugly, of course, but from a utilitarian point of view there were so many maids, butlers, footmen in houses that it didn't matter that it wanted two men to lift a chair. Nowadays this no longer holds true, so I think these heavy Victorian chairs will never be of any great monetary value.

But there are some Victorian chairs that are already desirable. One recalls the small rather pretty drawing-room chairs. They're nearly always in walnut and always on rather pretty Victorian-shaped cabriole legs, and there is a difference in the shape of the legs. It's still rather a sweet-flowing curve but there isn't the C scroll toe at the foot, nor is there the pad foot. It's a Victorian finish which is easily recognisable. These chairs stood in drawing-rooms, only for decorous tea party use, but nevertheless, when they are found today in a set of six or eight or ten, they do bring a very good price, simply because they are small and they're really not objectionable to live with. And again the small upholstered Victorian chairs, those which usually have what we call deep button-backs, have risen in price considerably of late, mainly, I think, because of their convenience for watching television.

It seems to me that the Chesterfield Suite with a large six-foot settee and large divan easy chairs has more or less gone out, because it's quite a major operation to move them so that everyone can see the screen. The Victorian upholstered easy chair with a rather low seat and shapely back, nicely sprung and upholstered, is quite comfortable, is easily movable by one person, and for modern ways spells the end of large upholstered settees.

Of course through all these periods right from the early Elizabethan chairs, which we didn't even mention, through Jacobean times and up to Regency chairs there are, and they are extremely rare, the corresponding type of chair made for children. They conform to all the known designs of their full-scale counterparts, their big-scale brothers of any period. For example a Charles II child's chair will have just the same cane panel back, usually the same cherub's head and all the attributes of the period, exactly the same except that the feet will be very much higher, the legs much taller. In other words it's a child's chair, but by its likeness in style to an adult's chair it can easily be identified and dated.

Tables

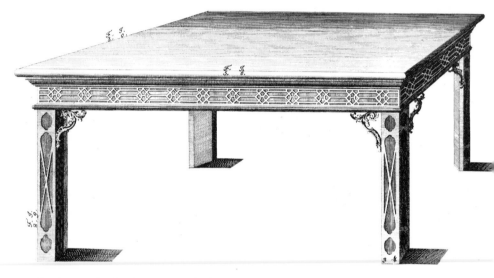

As I've said, the first type of dining-table was usually twenty or thirty feet long, because in those early days families took their meals with their staff, and so required long tables to seat forty, fifty or even more people. They were called refectory tables.

See these two illustrations, *38* and *39*: obviously they're not thirty feet long but they are a different type of refectory table in that they have draw-leaves. You know, it's said there's nothing new under the sun. This principle you see goes way back to 1580 and yet today you can buy a modern dining table which has just this same arrangement of leaves. The thick leaves pull out and drop down to lengthen the table. These two tables are exactly the same basically and yet they're very different. *38* is a little earlier for it has a flat frieze rail inlaid with a type of floral design in holly and bog-oak and it stands on four rather big, rather nice bulbous legs, carved with acanthus, and with square stretchers uniting them at floor level.

Now the second is also a draw-leaf refectory table but you see the flat frieze has given way to a moulded frieze deeply carved with gadroons, and you notice also that, although the four bulbous legs and stretchers are in exactly the same place, the conception is quite different. The legs are also carved on the top but with these sort of banana-like projections, matching, as it were, the gadroons around the frieze.

These are two good examples of tables made within twenty or thirty years of each other, basically the same and yet differing so much in detail. I believe the inlaid frieze indicates an earlier table because I recall visiting Hardwick Hall and seeing a games table somewhat similar in form to this draw-leaf table. It was inlaid with Bess of Hardwick's arms and undoubtedly was made about 1570 and had this early type of arabesque inlay on the top and round the friezes. So I imagine the flat inlaid box-like top is a little earlier than the ones with the gadroons.

Now *40* is a six-legged refectory table but compare the method of construction here. No work in the legs at all, thin turned baluster legs, plain again, with the square stretchers around them. The cost is nothing compared to the cost of the draw-leaf tables and this allows one to say that this is probably a table made for the servants' hall because the cost, even in those

38 Elizabethan draw-leaf refectory table, inlaid frieze, *c.*1590

39 Elizabethan draw-leaf refectory table, carved gadroons, *c.*1600

40 Jacobean refectory table, *c.*1640

41 Charles II coaching table, *c.* 1665

days, would be so much less than for *38* and *39* with all their detail.

It is, of course, remembered that originally the family and everyone took all their meals together. But this table is, to my mind, round about 1650 and this would be the sort of table, absolutely period but with no detail on the legs, just knocked up to stand in the servants' hall when the family took their meals by themselves in the so-called dining-room and left the staff to eat on their own. Usually one finds these tables made in oak or elm, of which there was plenty growing on the big estates.

41 shows a Charles II table. Let's imagine the date of this is about 1666, the time of the Great Fire of London, but it is extremely unusual. It stands, as one can see, on the spiral end-standards. And that, by the way, is what a Charles II spiral looks like, just like a barley-sugar twist. But this table is unusual in that it is large – it's four foot seven long in the bed, and it's in the form of an early English coaching-table. That just means a little tiny table, on end standards with a narrow bed, that people used to run out with to coaches when they arrived at coaching inns. Now this big table is

42 Charles II sidetable, *c.*1670   43 William and Mary half-round card-table, *c.*1695

in that form, but you notice the gates swing – they're pinned alternately on either side and each gate consists of three spirals. Notice also spiral stretchers. A great deal of work is required in making a spiral leg – it can't be turned, it has to be carved – and to my mind this table is very unusual because the gates are made with three upright spirals. You notice also another very rare feature. You can see the width of the bed in the bottom board. This bottom board is panelled, is about twelve inches wide and again is unusual. All this adds up to quite a nice, uncommon, early English oak table.

About this time – say 1650 – one feels the introduction of tea has taken the family into a smaller room to partake of it, and so has provided the need for smaller tables – tea-tables, small gate-leg tables and eventually larger gate-legs for use as dining-tables. It seems to me people were quick to adapt the gate-leg principle to other tables. I recall a walnut card-table of the William and Mary period, say somewhere round about 1695. *43* will show exactly what I mean. A half-round table, possibly has baize on it, more probably needlework under the two tops. But you notice the gate-leg principle at the back of it. Those two finials are actually the pins on which those two centre back-legs swing out and so when the flap is opened one virtually has a round table with the six legs absolutely equidistant, swung out at the back on this gate-leg principle.

Like the six-legged refectory table (*40*) *43* has a relatively plain baluster-turned leg, just with a sort of cotton-reel on the top but not much work there. But it has a very pretty under-stretcher nicely veneered in big curls—a lot of work. The shaped under-stretcher, of course, is absolutely typical of William and Mary and later of Queen Anne design. You see how it changed from the table illustrated in *42*. Here you have a walnut table with what we like to call barley-sugar-twist legs—Charles II, about 1670, with the spiral twists running all round instead of the square stretchers. This table, of course, is more usually found in oak. This one happens to be in walnut and is an extremely small size and, of course, is quite rare. You also get this early lovely barley-sugar twist on most of the supports of Charles II chairs.

44 Charles II
credence table, *c.*1665

You notice a curious combination in *44*. There you have a very similar table to the walnut one on the Carolean spiral legs (*42*). These spirals just differ a little in that in *44* they tend to be thinner at the top than they are at the bottom. They're actually tapered a little. But still the same idea, the barley-sugar twist, but in this table, known as a credence table, you have a combination of the side-table and a single gate at the back. This gate just swings from that central pin, opens out to carry the half-round top and so form a round table. These credence tables are so called because they're usually to be found in the chancels of churches. The wine, water and bread are put on them before they are consecrated.

45 shows another very good example of a Seventeenth-century credence table. We were talking of these gates which swing from the middle of the back. Here's a table on what is known as a triangular-shaped frame, with the half-round folding tops, a gate at the back and just the same sort of leg as on all chairs of the period, all baluster-turned. Square stretcher, square bottom-board to the gate, taking the place of the stretcher-rails. You see there is something attractive in a table like this, because it is so simple and yet the outline of it and the balance and the form of it are just marvellous. Here is a plain oak table, no enrichments whatever, its attractiveness only in the line and the shape of the baluster leg. This is a true guide to a decent piece.

You notice the brass ring handles on *42*; the ring of the handle is held by a type of split-pin principle – two wires, fixed to the ring, go through a hole in the drawer front and one is bent up and one is bent down. Sometimes the wires were secured by a tack being driven into the other side of the drawer. But one can easily visualise how, with heavy weights in the drawer, a good tug on the ring handle would immediately pull the wires straight through the front.

This seems to be the reason why so many of the older pieces of furniture lack their original handles. It isn't until you get into the Eighteenth century that you get handles fixed by a nut and bolt principle, and bear in mind that even when they fixed a handle, they were so concerned with the way in which the job was finished that on a superb piece of furniture you'll find the nut will be counter-sunk into the back of the drawer-front, so that anyone putting their hands inside a drawer to remove linen or whatnot cannot possibly scratch them on the rough sides of the nut.

45 Jacobean credence table, *c.*1670

Referring to *43* again. Here you'll notice that the frieze of the table and the top too, I'm sure, is in fact veneered. This William and Mary period was productive of some of the finest veneered furniture, with picked curls of walnut wood cut down near the branches or low in the roots to give it the figure. It was cut into veneers to give a better effect as the trunk of a walnut tree is rather severely plain. You'll recall William and Mary oyster-shell cabinets in walnut and laburnum, so beautifully made and so very attractive in their veneered finish. It will be appreciated that the plain walnut is in the trunk of the tree and the so-called oyster is simply a cross-section of a small branch of wood.

Incidentally at this time, round about 1695, one first meets the mention of the word 'cabinet-maker'. Up to then they had all been joiners and picture-frame makers, but German and Dutch cabinet-makers came to England and settled in Norfolk during William III's reign. Without question they made some extremely fine pieces, no doubt enjoying to the full the process of veneering things with these pretty, grained woods. You know, these veneers would be cut by these cabinet-makers themselves, from say the lower butt end of the trunk of a walnut tree. This veneer is known as saw-cut and is about one eighth of an inch thick when it is cut by hand.

Today, of course, the veneers are cut with machines and are referred to

46 Chippendale two-flap dining-table, *c.*1760

as knife-cut. They're so thin that it is virtually impossible to do any cleaning up or sandpapering of their surface before one rubs completely through it. I've even watched my father cut veneers with a panel-saw. It's rather a precarious job because it is, as I say, a rather large piece of wood, perhaps three feet by two – a big lump of a trunk of a tree – and it's necessary to put your knee on it and start work with the saw, and you saw and saw and saw. Believe me, it's one of the easiest things in the world to take a piece out of your knee while you're sawing the wood. As a matter of fact I was put to this task, and, although my father didn't take a piece out of his knee, I most certainly did and bear the scar to this very day.

I hope to give you a lot of tips – hints if you like – whereby one can easily recognise a period, and in this respect it is surprising how one can judge a table by the different mouldings upon the top. For example, all walnut mouldings are cross-grained, they're in quite different form from the later Eighteenth-century mahogany mouldings. The same also applies to cock-beads on chests-of-drawers and cabinets. Here again the position of the cock-beads can often dictate the age of the article. You see, these cabinet-makers employed the same type of work on a moulding for most pieces of furniture that were made at the same date, so that on a Charles II table you would expect to find a moulding somewhat similar to one around a cabinet and most certainly on a mirror frame. The same theme or method of construction seems to go right through all walnut; then when the introduction of mahogany comes, the whole idea alters, the method of making a moulding changes. And here again the selfsame thing applies, you get the same mouldings on mahogany chests, mahogany tables, mahogany mirrors, mahogany anything – all worked now in long-grain.

Now we come to the walnut period, about 1700 and for the next twenty or thirty years. Gate-legs were made but now a new design came in, probably for the same reason that people don't like gate-legs all that much today, because there are so many legs and stretchers to dodge when you sit at one. This next dining-table was made in walnut – in English walnut and in French red walnut – and in all the other woods and also after about 1730 in mahogany. It's a kind of gate-leg table, not really a gate-leg because it has no gates along the sides. The legs themselves move. One leg on each side swings around an angle of 90° and so holds the flap. So you have just the same table-top – a big oval two-flap top supported by four legs, usually cabriole legs in walnut, and this goes on way into the Eighteenth century, changing from walnut into mahogany.

46 shows an ordinary two-flap Chippendale mahogany dining-table with an octagonal top, a top just cut into this octagonal shape with quite an ordinary moulding round the sides. All the work, as with so many of Chippendale's chairs, is reserved for the legs. And the top's raised on four cabriole legs, the deep carved acanthus leaf going from the top of the leg to quite half-way down. It has shoulder brackets, also carved, carrying the same design of the acanthus. And there is that lovely ball-and-claw foot at the bottom, where you can almost see the strain of those knuckles on the claw. No shortage of wood here, you see. No question of this being carved up from a table with a little tiny pad foot, but a massive great lump of wood on the bottom. Beautifully carved and made to represent this claw foot really gripping that ball. This is quite a nice type of table. It has certain drawbacks of course; can't be enlarged. Just all right for people to sit at when they are all in set places. This perhaps is why this type of table has gone out of favour somewhat.

Then for some reason, I don't know why, the whole thing changes once more and you get dining-tables made in sections. Now you get a dining-

47 Sheraton 3-section dining-table, *c*.1790

table standing on fourteen legs (47). This time they're square, taper legs. This three-section mahogany dining-table – they're always in mahogany – has a two-flap centre with half-round ends. It's a separate half-round table which fits on either end and these tables do carry extra leaves and can go up to ten, twelve, thirteen, fourteen feet long when they're all assembled together. The legs on the two-flap centre swing out in exactly the same way as the earlier table through an angle of 90° and support the flaps. When these flaps are up, the half-round table is added to each end. Invariably, nowadays, one finds perhaps one or two of the half-round ends used as dressing-tables.

Of course they are big tables and they went out of favour in about 1780–90. I imagine simply for the same reason as the gate-legs – that they aren't too practical. They're quite all right to sit ten or twelve people at if you space them exactly so that they all dodge the legs, but jolly awkward if you want to get one or two extra people in and you have to squeeze them up a bit. In the old days you got ladies trying to cuddle straight taper legs with long skirts, they didn't know whether to sit sideways in their dining-chairs, or cuddle the leg, or what.

Of course, with its extra leaves this table was no doubt made to meet many different requirements because, you see, you could dispense with the centre table and you could put the two half-round ends together to make a round table. This would be a dining-table which would seat, quite comfortably, six or eight. Or you could use them as separate tables. You could also use the two half-round ends with one of the extra leaves to make a sort of oval table. But the size of the top would then be something like six to seven foot long – just a nice size perhaps for eight to ten people. On the other hand, you could scrap that whole idea and you could use just the centre two-flap table which would be enough for eight people to sit at very comfortably. If you wanted more people in, well then you could amalgamate the whole lot and so get a long big dining-table with its extra leaves but unfortunately still with those fourteen legs.

These very big diners have mostly been split up over the years. Now, I'll give you a tip. This is a table which has two deep flaps going down to the ground. The flaps end no more than six or nine inches off the ground. You can always tell whether or not they're part of a bigger table because all you need to do is to run your hand along the square edge of the flaps and you will probably find two or three little slots. This is a give-away, because they are obviously the slots that the tongues on the inside edges of the half-round ends fitted into to join up the whole table and keep it absolutely level. If you don't feel the slots it may be because someone has reduced the leaves by about half an inch to remove this tell-tale sign, but with these tables the middles aren't all that valuable and I doubt whether people would bother to do that.

And you see, the dates of these three types of tables sort of spread all through the Eighteenth century. You get the first type of drop-leaf table with the corner legs swinging (but not a gate-leg) from about 1700 to the middle of the century. Overlapping with them from about 1740 you get the square drop-leaf tables with the big flaps and separate half-round ends. They go on to about 1780 when, as I've said, owing to their awkwardness for seating they gradually went out of favour.

Now come the pedestal dining-tables (48) dating from about 1780. These pedestal tables are called pillar-diners and were probably the most popular type of dining-table ever made. The most unusual type stands on a pair of quite separate columns, normally with tripod or quadruple-shaped and spreading feet. The point about these tables is that they will carry an extra leaf. You get a two-pillar with an extra leaf, no legs to dodge at all, and these tables go larger with three pillars and four pillars.

Both types of table were made for a while, but there is one quick way of telling when you've got an early pedestal table as against one made way into the Nineteenth century. You have the central column quite prettily turned in both cases. When the tripod or quadruple legs come straight off the column (as with the sofa-table 63 on p. 134), this dates the table as being between 1780 to 1800. When the legs have bumps on them, or what is known in the trade as having toothache, they're most certainly in the Nineteenth century.

48 shows this point well. It's a three-pillar dining-table, but there's the rather heavy turned pedestal column and the rather nasty quadruple supports. You see it has these 'toothache' bumps on the knees, and it shows how rather nasty these pedestals can get when they get round the corner and into the first twenty or thirty years of the Nineteenth century. It's a fact that in my lifetime I've helped my father cut these tables up because at one time about forty years ago they refused to sell; and it was

48 Late Georgian 3-pillar dining-table, *c.*1820

nothing for me to be asked if I would rip seven or eight inches off the edge of one because it was just the right colour and would so easily make into bracket feet to go on a straight-front chest-of-drawers. Funnily enough, the straight-front chest-of-drawers is now only worth about £30 but a table like the one you see in the photograph is probably worth six hundred or more. It's a curious thing how fashions dictate, but I have really cut up the tops of these tables simply because they were worth about two or three pounds and no one would buy them. Yet today, as you see, the table is worth twenty times as much as the chest.

Of course there's one thing to remember when you're looking at these tables. Here's a Nineteenth-century table which can carry one extra leaf in between each of the three sections, so this table obviously carries two extra leaves. It's not until much later in the Nineteenth century, perhaps towards the middle of it, that you get the desire for even bigger tables and the introduction of dining-tables which had an extending frame, so that any number of extra leaves could be put into them. They had a handle at one end which turned, tightened the whole thing up, and made the top rigid. So none of these tables on extending frames can be any earlier than William IV.

I know of a six-pillar dining-table which incidentally was found in separate pieces all over the house, and the sixth part I found being used in the laundry where the maids were actually ironing clothes on it. The longer, the bigger they are, the more pedestals they stand on, so much the more valuable do they become. And all these sections, each supporting a big top, can all be joined together with an extra leaf going in between each pedestal support. So you can see a six-pedestal diner could easily stretch to about twenty-four feet – and, as I say, no legs to dodge.

So much for dining-tables. Now we go back to William Kent, the first man to have a big influence on English furniture design. He went to Italy about 1710, studied architecture there for ten years, returned to England and not only designed fine houses, but also designed some furniture to go in them. But he never seemed to get the Italian baroque idea out of his mind, because although he designed large houses fit only for noblemen, he also designed furniture for such houses, and *49* clearly shows the point I'm trying to make. That is a wonderful table – without question a wonderful table. But in fact I expect that table is at least seven foot long and has a scagliola marble top. It would be very, very heavy to lift and move about.

49 William Kent carved gesso hall table, *c.*1730

50 William Kent
gesso table, c.1720

Impossible for anyone living in any house other than a large mansion to accommodate it. You've noticed the enormous deep Italianate frieze of great sunflowers and scrolls, the tremendous mask-head from which it all seems to emerge in the centre of the frieze, the extremely bold, but nevertheless pretty, broken S-shaped legs. You can see the width of it on the one which is canted to the front of the photograph.

50 shows a very good example of a William Kent gesso table. This is completely gilt, gilt all over. It's not so heavy as the great hall table, with that enormous frieze and that tremendous mask. But you see the masks are reproduced now on the corners of the legs. And the frieze is quietened down a bit. This table would be made in pine – the whole of it in pine. And then it would be covered in gesso, which is the Italian word for the preparation, somewhat like plaster of Paris, which is brushed onto the carved pine of that table. Brushed on, dried, brushed on again, to give it some body, so that the gold leaf will adhere better. The top you can see is carved all over and would probably be all in gesso. This would have this sort of plaster of Paris built right up on a plain piece of wood and that itself would be carved. The top would not necessarily be carved in the wood, but certainly carved in the gesso and of course gilt all over. These tables are

51 Adam sideboard, c.1780

scarce. This one would date from about 1715-20, and, being this size and of much finer proportion than *49*, would be a more desirable type of article. Incidentally, this was another table shown on *Going for a Song*.

In passing it might be worth drawing attention to the cabriole front legs. You see under the mask there is this large dropping acanthus leaf, carved in rather high relief, and then coming up from the scroll-toe, the pointed toe at the bottom, up comes another acanthus leaf in high relief again, as it were coming up to meet the one which is coming down. A detail like this adds greatly to the value of the table. Such a leg as that is so much better than a plain straightforward gesso cabriole leg.

These are good examples of what Chippendale in the first place went to work on, lightening such furniture; and later we come along to people like Robert Adam who turned this sort of hall table into a sideboard or a serving-table such as you see in *51*. They are absolutely different. The design, of course, has changed tremendously. You see that wonderful frieze, this neo-classic design of Robert Adam on the frieze. There is the urn in the centre, the swags of laurel, the oval patera, so prettily carved all along the frieze. What a difference there is between these two friezes – the William Kent and the Robert Adam.

You know, it's a remarkable thing that Adam should introduce this neo-classic period. All this business of the oval patera, the swags of flowers, the drapery, the urns, the goats' heads, the rams' heads, the bluebell drops, became greatly copied in other media. For instance Josiah Wedgwood and some of his jasper ware. Some of the jugs he made in that jasper ware, really wonderful. But they're just copies of this new neo-classic design. Derby porcelain. Chelsea Derby, painted in that wonderful green. All the borders nothing but swags of laurel. Again, cribs from Adam's design. And of course silversmiths. From about 1780 onwards nearly all the borders are engraved, pierced with little urns, little swags, little oval patera, exactly the same idea running right through all the things that were made by these good houses and good craftsmen from 1780 to about 1800.

Now we come on to talking about card-tables. Curiously enough 52 and 53 are photographed on snow. This may seem a queer thing to do but circumstances forced us to do it. Do you remember that hard winter of 1947? Well, we were called to sell the contents of a house some three miles from Cheltenham and I was absolutely amazed, going down the main road sign-posted to Warwick, to find at least a fifteen or twenty foot high wall of snow, making it absolutely impossible for me to get to this house. Of course there were the usual complications, the property had been sold and we had a completion date when the new owner could quite rightfully claim to go into this house free of all its furniture. So, after about a week or ten days of waiting, a passageway was cut through this great wall of snow for something like half a mile and I did get to the house and, because time was pressing, it was necessary to carry these two tables out of the house, stand them on the snow-covered lawn, and photograph them.

This was an extremely fine old Cotswold mansion. It had been Indianised, as it were, by the former owner who had returned from India and maybe had built towers resembling the various minarets and things that he was so used to seeing in India. They'd sort of Indianised a lovely Cotswold stone house – Carolean or even earlier, I suppose. It boasted Cromwell's bullets in a very heavy iron-studded door and it really was quite an extraordinary house. This house was genuinely old and as I was very pushed for time in preparing the catalogue, I had to take my wife and my younger daughter with me to help by fetching out all china and glass from cupboards.

Freezing cold in this house, one Saturday we three arrived and I put my wife and daughter in a very large china pantry and asked them if they would bring out all the china–dinner, tea and dessert services–from a long range of cupboards. I left them and went to work in another part of the house. I'm now told that my wife said to my daughter, 'Close the door, Anne'. This was an oak-panelled door with a Norfolk latch. 'Close the door, Anne' she says. My daughter goes and shuts the door; it opens. 'I thought I told you to close that door, why don't you do as you're told?' The child closes the door but once more it opens. Mrs Negus, losing her temper, says, 'Oh, you're useless'. She walks across, closes the door and takes particular care to pull down the Norfolk latch with her hands as she shuts the door, thereby making no mistake that it is closed. It opens once more. My

52 Chippendale card-table, cluster-column legs, c.1760

wife says, 'Come along, Anne, we're off!' And out of the house they marched and nothing would induce them ever again to go back in it to help me with my catalogue.

The sale, of course, took place and *52* and *53* are actually two card-tables that were in this house. Absolutely genuine in every respect, un-doubtedly made during the third quarter of the Eighteenth century, and probably never had another home. These tables are fairly similar in that they have a leg at each corner and the folding double top lined with baize. But you see how the one differs from the other. All the work in *52* is contained chiefly in the legs. This type of Chinese Chippendale leg is known as a cluster-column leg. It is actually three long, turned spindles with those rings at intervals stuck together to form a three-sided square leg – a cluster column. You see it has the influence of what we call a Chippendale scroll bracket. That C scroll pierced bracket there adds to the quality of this table, and it braces the corner from the top of the leg across to the frieze of the table.

Now if you look at both photographs you will see that the leg on *53* is so different, it is just a square chamfered piece of wood with a moulding worked down the front edges and no real craftsmanship required in pre-paring it. Nothing like the cost of the cluster-column leg. On the other hand where the first table has what we call a 'blind' fret frieze, the second table is similar except that the fret frieze is pierced right through with this Eighteenth-century gothic design. You'll notice that the tops of the first table are quite plain at the edges but those of the second one have really cost a lot more money. Both its edges are beautifully carved with flower-heads and acanthus.

So on the one table, you see, a lot of money went on the legs, and on the other one a good deal of money went on the actual edges of the top. You notice, too, that the first table is of a serpentine outline but has square corners, whereas *53* is just a plain serpentine all the way round. Some people call these tables butterfly-top tables because of a butterfly-wing appearance when they're opened. Actually I like to think of them more as just a plain straightforward serpentine outline.

Most card-tables work on the same swing-leg principle as the dining-tables I've described. Of course you see some of these card-tables looking a bit peculiar when they're open. Now, an ordinary two-flap diner does

53 Chippendale card-table, *c*.1765

match up – when the leaves are up. You do have four spaced legs. Two legs move through an angle of 90° and the thing looks right. But with a card-table usually only one leg swings, through the same 90°, and you get a queer looking thing, you get, as it were, a square table with one leg at each of three corners and an odd one sort of poking out somewhere close to one of the others.

You can also get two hinged legs but these look knock-kneed when the table's opened, because there again, when the table is closed you have a leg at each corner. When the table is opened, in the front of the table you still have a leg at each corner because these are fixed. You go round the back of it and each leg that formerly was at the corner has now moved to some angle like 75° off the square and they look funny.

There is a nicer type of card-table which opens to support the flap, and this is what we call a table with a concertina action. This word concertina describes perfectly the intricate movement. When you pull the back of the table out, the sides (which are hinged) unfold to make a straight edge and a complete support for the opened table, leaving a leg at each corner as before – and these look absolutely grand. And another thing too, always

54 Adam card-table, c.1785

55 Hepplewhite enclosed dressing-table, *c.*1780

with a concertina action one seems to get a table of superb quality, and a lot of antiques have to be judged entirely on quality – the quality of the workmanship and all that. The art of a practical man making a concertina-table has to be of a much higher standard than the art required to make a card-table with one or two swinging legs.

You see now the change which has taken place with 54, an Adam table. Possibly that's a kindness to call it by Robert Adam because it's still a little bit on the heavy side, but it is in satinwood, which first suggests Adam, and is a half-round card-table. The others were serpentine, this is half-round, has a two-flap top and stands just on plain simple legs – the date of this one being something like 1780–5, the other two probably 1760–70. Now with this table there's no work in the legs; there's a veneered half-round frieze in satinwood, it's true, but all the real work's on the top. A lovely floral marquetry band, cross-grained border and the satinwood inlaid in segments all pointing back to a big shell in the centre of the back of the table. The top of this table is really very fine.

You will perhaps realise, looking at the photographs, how you get the same influence showing throughout all these mahogany tables, doing all sorts of different things, the legs either being square or cabriole or cluster-column or tapering. The trend of the whole transition period from say 1740 right up to 1800 by each successive designer or cabinet-maker was to make the things lighter in appearance. It happens on an early Chippendale card-table which would have heavy cabriole legs with ball-and-claw feet. There's a lot of work in making a cabriole leg, carving it, fining down the wood to make that pretty shape, and Chippendale saw the wisdom of reducing the cost of such tables, keeping the tops much the same but dispensing with the costly cabriole and standing them up on square legs. You see, too, the adaptations of these square legs, how he became influenced by the Chinese and went to town with legs like cluster-columns or of bamboo pattern.

Now he was followed, of course, by a very fine chairmaker, George Hepplewhite, and, of course, by Thomas Sheraton. It seems to me that they all cribbed the designs, the one from the other, but at least George Hepplewhite was honest about it. For they all wrote books, they all published catalogues of their designs, the first man ever to do it, of course, being Chippendale. All the others copied him, but Hepplewhite in the preface to his book says that there's nothing new in it, and that he's simply taken existing designs and lightened them.

And a supreme example of this lightening of the line of a table seems to me to be most apparent in 55. This is a little Hepplewhite table with a rising top. It's not a card-table—it's actually a little fitted dressing-table. You see it still retains the serpentine outline of the top, still veneered in a sort of radial design, triangular panels going into the centre. That top lifts up and inside are little box-topped compartments and possibly a small mirror. But the point I'm trying to make is the degree to which George Hepplewhite has thinned these legs. Here you have a perfect example of what, forty years before, was probably a heavy cabriole leg with ball-and-claw feet. Now it's turned itself under the inspiration of this fine cabinet-maker into the thinnest of cabriole legs with the tiniest of pointed toes. If he'd reduced it any further there really would have been no leg at all, and yet look how pretty, how extremely pretty, this table is.

And this recalls to my mind a criticism levelled at Robert Adam and George Hepplewhite by Horace Walpole. He went to see some of Robert Adam's new designs and remarked that he had a great liking for the heavy baroque furniture of William Kent (49), adding, 'From Kent's mahogany we are dwindled to Adam's filigree; grandeur and simplicity are not in the fashion'. Now this little late Eighteenth-century table, although it's Hepplewhite, reflects what the man meant, how, compared with the solid oak tables of about 1700, the solid walnut William and Mary card-tables, the heavier early pre-Chippendale tables, how this table seems almost to be dancing around the room.

It's a curious thing, you know, how Chippendale was influenced in a lot of his later designs by the Chinese while George Hepplewhite was influenced by the French. This little table, this enclosed dressing-table, surely shows French influence creeping into its design.

Now let's turn to another table, also Eighteenth-century and in mahogany. The table commonly known as a tripod table. You see here again in 56 you have a very plain, round tip-up table-top on a nicely carved stem. The photograph shows the long acanthus carved three parts of the way down the leg and a rather nice carved ball-and-claw foot. And on the other hand 57 (p. 121) shows a very similar sort of table and yet it's so different. Here is the plainest of tripods with all the money spent on this very

56 Chippendale tripod table, *c.*1770

unusual and very nice top. Known, of course, as a decafoil with those ten lobes around the edges, and curiously enough this table is Eighteenth-century–I would think about 1780. All that ornament in the top is in brass, beautifully inlaid brass, of absolute supreme quality. What a contrast in the two tables. The one with all the money on the base, the other on the top.

As a general rule the better sort of tip-up table always has the top clipping down onto what we call a birdcage fitting, which holds the top

119

very firm and rigid when it's down. By the way, to my way of thinking the top in 57 is up but that in 56 is down. Another thing well worth noticing concerns the carving of the feet. Where the pad feet are plain, occasionally, in order to give the table a more important appearance, the feet are later carved into ball-and-claw feet and these two photographs clearly show the amount of wood required in the first instance to cut a genuine ball-and-claw foot. You see in 57, no matter how nicely this pad was carved into a ball-and-claw, it would to my mind, always appear very skimpy, skinny and shallow. The foot on 56 is so large by comparison and, remember, a good deal of that wood has been cut away in order to produce that original ball-and-claw. If an original pad foot has been recarved later to give it more class you can always recognise it by the skimpiness—there's just nothing like enough wood for the foot to have been done properly. It gives itself away.

You notice on the carved tripod table 56 the fluted vase-turned stem. This is a good type of stem. It changes considerably in the Nineteenth century. When you get round the corner after 1800 this stem, instead of being rather pretty and attractive, becomes heavy and has many turned collars on it. The vase disappears and from this stem alone one can date a table either before or after 1800.

Coming to the next table (58, p. 123). Here you have what will be recognised by everyone as another tip-up table with a pie-crust top. This pie-crust is rather interesting in so far as plain table-tops, such as we saw in 56, are sometimes turned into pie-crusts. The way to tell when this has happened is fairly simple. The original table is put in a lathe and as it were reduced down. The edge, the pie-crust edge, is then actually carved out of solid. Now if 56 had to be turned into a pie-crust, it would need to have an inch or so of wood planted on top of its existing edge so that it could be reduced and carved into this pie-crust form. So on original pie-crust tables there are no joins at all around the pie-crust edge. A joint showing there would immediately give the game away.

You see the quality of the mahogany in that table (58), that very fine grain. Well, this table we once had for sale. It was standing as tables normally do with the pie-crust top down. Seeing what nice quality it was I decided to photograph it and I have a weakness for these tables when the tops are turned up as you see it in the photograph. It was photo-

graphed just like it is and, shall I say unfortunately, left in that position. The owner, walking through his house, saw the table and said, 'Where did this table come from?', and of course I told him it was his and he said, 'Well, I don't ever remember seeing a table like this about the house.' I then put the top down and he said, 'Oh yes, of course, I remember it. Oh well, now I've seen it with the top up I don't wish to sell it.' And so although we almost had it for sale, we didn't get it and I trust the owner enjoys it very much to this very day!

Of course there are many tripod tables about that are marriages, which simply means that an old round top from some other table is planted on, or married to, a tripod base. You will see in each of these photographs that the diameter of the top practically equals the width of the spread of the legs. It's curious this, how this should be. When you get a top which is much larger in diameter than the spread, the thing looks ridiculous, it's at once top-heavy. When you get one whose top is small by comparison to the spread of the legs, it really looks tiny and absurd. The ideal thing is for the top practically to equal the spread.

It's a curious thing about tripod supports. Three in one, the three legs on the one stem – this likeness to the Trinity. Curious to me that this is the only table that you cannot rock. It is impossible to rock anything which stands on three legs. You can have them on four or more and they twist and rock about all over the place but a three-legged table stands absolutely and supremely firm.

You might well wonder why anyone would wish to turn 56 with its plain top into a table similar to 58 with the pie-crust top. This is simply a question of money. A pie-crust top is much rarer than a plain table. 57, of course, is also rare. The brass inlay in fact makes this extremely rare. Many of these tables with lobed edges have the arcs around the edge continuing into circles, so that on this table you would have ten circles leaving another round in the middle. Then this table would be properly called a supper-table, because you could set up on it eleven big round dishes filled with fruit, hors-d'oeuvres and so on. But this is only half inclined to be a supper-table. It isn't one and is rare in its own right with the brass inlay.

59 is a rather unusual urn-stand or possibly vase-stand. You see, if you look at this with 52, it's obviously Chippendale. Here you have the same type of cluster-column legs, except in this instance they have all been

58 Chippendale table with pie-crust border, *c.* 1770

glued up very close together. On the card-table in *52* they were open clusters, here they are absolutely tight together. This again is a blind fret frieze, and where some of the fret is missing it clearly shows that it was

59 Chippendale vase-stand, c.1770

applied and not carved out of the solid. Again we get the serpentine outline. This is Chippendale about 1770. I think it might be a vase-stand rather than a tea-urn stand because of the sunken rim in the centre of the table which seems to indicate that something with a round – possibly unglazed – foot-rim and base stood thereon. This could well have been an urn but usually urn-stands have a small slide fixed in a member of the moulding, so that it can be pulled out to rest the cup and saucer on when tea is required from the urn.

Once again, on this small table, we've got the tripod supports, not quite the same as on the pie-crust tables because they don't have a common stem – just these three rather stout legs. But no movement whatever, as firm as a rock. I'm pretty sure it's absolutely safe to say that one does not find these cluster-column legs, be they pierced or solid, anywhere in the Nineteenth century. When they're old, they're almost certainly in the last third of the Eighteenth. All such little tables are valuable. They're rare and they're highly desirable, because unfortunately in these days it seems that, following every death in a family, people move to something just a little smaller.

There is no staff available as there was in Victorian times so that one is obliged to furnish one's home with the absolute essentials, be they very nice and attractive, but no fussy little supplementary things, everything there for a purpose. And of course with so many small town houses or flats in London, whose owners have a liking for antiques, you can see why such small things as this table are highly desirable. My wife bought a small coffee-table in beech, absolutely modern, a little tiny table on a tripod, which I hated because it was supposed to be made of walnut but it was in fact beech. She liked it, I hated it. Eventually I had my own way, it was put into a sale and made exactly £3 more than the table could be bought for in one of the Cheltenham shops.

I come now to a common form of table, a Pembroke table, but how different these tables can be. Look at *60*. This is a Sheraton table, very clean in outline, nice sharp lines about it, but so simple, in rosewood with a drawer, two flaps of course. You know that a Pembroke table is simply a two-flap table with the flaps hinged down the long side. Sofa-tables are somewhat similar but they always have their flaps hanging off the short sides. But this Pembroke table you see in rosewood has a cross-banded top, just fitted with a drawer, square taper legs, inlaid with a white stringing.

I imagine a cabinet-maker would perhaps have a weakness for making Pembroke tables. He might first think of a table such as this one—a table of simple outlines on a square frame with the two flaps on square taper legs and a drawer; perhaps the first one would be completely plain, then he might make another with cross-banding like this on the top. Then another with similar cross-banding to the top but going to the extra trouble of veneering the edge—and you notice the edges of this table are also veneered cross-wise. Then perhaps after a lot of practice, as it were, in making these he might go on to a table such as *61*.

60 Sheraton Pembroke table, *c.*1805

Here you see an oval table with a moulded edge, the same thing in principle as *60*, a leg at each corner, two flaps along the long side and a drawer.
But look at the enormous trouble that this man has been to in making this
table. There's a very large oval medallion inlaid in the bed of the table at
the top, and you notice the flap (both flaps are the same) – the satinwood
inlay is in segments like bat's wings running towards a central point where
there is another half oval shell, the border again cross-grained.

61 Hepplewhite Pembroke table, *c.*1785

It has a similar type of leg to *60* except that it also has a white line on the edge and is cross-banded, and the drawer-front veneered in a number of vertical flutes, probably in mahogany, on satinwood framing. There are two flower-head medallions on the tops of the square taper legs and you notice with this table that the frame carries the same outline as the top. This is quite an important thing when one considers Pembroke tables.

Tables with oval tops are very much better when they sit on a frame which carries the same outline. That means so to say, when they are fitted with a drawer that has a bow front rather than sitting on a square frame. You'll notice also the manner in which the flaps hang down, or are fixed to the bed – the centre portion of each table. They are hung with what is known as a rule-joint. This rule-joint in itself means an awful lot of work because, if you could imagine taking that end flap off, you would see a moulding which is absolutely similar to the moulding running round the edge of the table above the drawer. The flap, of course, has a complementary concave moulding that fits snugly round its convex opposite number. Nothing can get through this joint and when the flap is raised it just has that extra firmness as compared with a flap hung with square edges and only supported on three hinges.

Rule-joints on tables like this or on any other piece of furniture are sure signs of the quality and skill of the cabinet-maker. I'm sure if you pulled out the drawer on either of these tables, you would find that the drawer sides were nothing like a quarter of an inch thick. They would be thin, beautifully dovetailed together, and this again is a good sign of the best English cabinet work.

To digress for a second, one can nearly always recognise a foreign piece of furniture, particularly when it is fitted with drawers, because the method of construction of the drawers usually demanded that the sides were quite a half-inch thick. English cabinet-makers now, the thinner the sides they could use and still maintain the strength, so much the better they liked it.

Of course, this may sound very confusing but I am really only talking of the finest English cabinet-makers of the late Eighteenth century. One can think back to earlier English tables in oak or elm, tables of the Seventeenth century, these of course being made with thick drawer sides and often with side-runners. In Queen Anne walnut, too, where one really meets cabinet-makers at work in England for the first time, in a walnut bureau-

62 Sheraton Pembroke table, *c.*1790

bookcase of finest quality, the drawer sides would also be thin. It's a curious thing what a high standard cabinet work reached in England all through the Eighteenth century, and particularly during the last quarter. Especially at this time one notices the beautifully made dovetails.

129

On the other hand one finds good period Dutch pieces of furniture with the drawers nailed together. In fact this is something I look for at once if I have reason to think a piece of furniture might be Dutch. It's bound to have the drawer sides nailed. Why, with Dutch and German cabinet-makers operating in England in William and Mary's reign and a bit later, before the advent of the great English cabinet-makers, why this practice of nailing drawer sides wasn't carried out in England I shall never know. It remains a fact that apparently in England this high standard was set which everyone conformed to.

But on the Continent, particularly perhaps in Italy, the workmanship of the cabinet-makers was really poor by comparison. When one generalises and talks about cabinet-makers on the Continent, of course, one mustn't forget that the French *Maîtres Ébénistes* were absolutely supreme. Perhaps this was why men of the calibre of Chippendale and Hepplewhite were attracted to the French for some of their designs. I mean particularly George Hepplewhite who, as I've said, was greatly influenced by the work of these men in Louis XVI's reign, and I feel sure it must have been their superb craftsmanship that attracted him.

62 is another ordinary two-flap Pembroke table with the usual drawer but made in satinwood. Of course the satinwood was used as a veneer, as you can see if you look closely at the top edge. But look at the quality of that, the figuring in the grain of the top, just fine cabinet-making again. Once more a chap being determined to make what is a nice table.

A cross-grain border of kingwood all around the edge, and not much else to say about it except that it just stands out as a table of supreme quality. The usual form, you see, raised on the four square taper legs, a little black line running down the extreme edge on all four sides. On each corner there is just that little black line going down once more to show a man being very careful about what he made, down even to the brass castors underneath, just for easy pushing in a room. The drawer oak-lined, nice wainscot oak. The drawer sides not more than a quarter of an inch thick, and of course the drawer completely unstained. It all adds up to a table made in the Eighteenth century, brand new then.

Of course, these Pembroke tables were made over a long period and whilst the form of their top remains the same in so far as they usually have two flaps and a drawer, the supports change considerably and after

1800–say the first forty years of the Nineteenth century–you get the legs taken away and you get them raised on a central pillar. Sometimes these pillars are quite clumsy because here we're getting along into the beginning of George IV, later still William IV, when the furniture becomes increasingly more heavy. Heavy pillars, a nasty type of quadruple support (often with toothache bumps like the dining table *48*) and a distinct change from these very attractive Eighteenth-century tables.

By the way, you can also learn to recognise the date of a piece of furniture from the drawer. In *60* and *61* the grain of the bottom board, in either case, would run crosswise whereas in a drawer made before about 1730 the grain would almost invariably run lengthwise. And in any table made *after* 1800 or thereabouts, inside the drawer there would be a half-round bead down the sides and this is a thing to look for. Anywhere you see a half-round bead inside a drawer, running down the sides, this I am sure is certainly Nineteenth-century.

It's a curious thing how one acquires knowledge and how many years might elapse before one is ever able to turn that knowledge into something practical. Over forty years ago I was asked to go and prepare an inventory in a house just outside Reading. Usually when one visits such houses, having met the owner one is asked some pertinent questions about a piece of furniture. In other words you are tried out. You're asked about a certain piece about which the owner would know all the answers, and in this way the owner can satisfy himself that at least you're a person with some sort of knowledge.

I was asked to accompany the owner through this mansion to a small boudoir where she showed me a French table. 'What do you think of that?' she said. I said, 'Well, quite honestly I've no idea. We walked past a lot of English furniture and you haven't asked me any questions about this, but you bring me up here and show me a French table about which I know nothing. Obviously I must get some help. I must get a man to come and tell me all about it.' 'You do that,' she said, 'and I would like to meet him.' So in due course two of us are met. We walk through the house to this very room but what a difference in the approach between the knowledgeable man and myself.

He doesn't even enter the room, he stays in the doorway and says, 'Good Lord, there are only seven tables like this known in the world.

131

There's one in the Louvre and one in Versailles and two in the British Museum, and just think I should come into this house and see one like it.' 'Yes,' she said. He looked at it and said, 'I wonder where it's signed?' 'Oh,' she said, 'I can show you.' 'Phew,' he said, 'I don't want you to show me, because I know the man that made this table, this was made by Roger Vandercruse.'[1] He then walked into the room for the first time, up to the table, ran his hand all across it and said, 'Oh yes, there's the signature, it's worth two-and-a-half-thousand.' 'Thank you very much,' she said and obviously, collectively at least, we'd passed the test.

Outside the house on the gravel path I say to this man, 'Charlie, I'm supposed to be making this inventory, I haven't got a clue what you two have been talking about.' 'But', he said, 'you stood there, you heard the price.' I said, 'Yes.' He said, 'If I send you a full description of it, then, you can type that and put that price in and that'll be right.' I said, 'O.K.' He got in his car apparently to drive off, but he got out again and came back to me, and bear in mind this was, as I say, over forty years ago. He said, 'You're only a young man.' I said, 'Yes.' He said, 'If I were to tell you something about that table would you remember it?' So I said, 'I would.' 'You wouldn't be offended?' 'No.' Then he said, 'Did you know it was French?' And I said 'Yes.' 'Did you know it was old?' I said, 'Yes.' 'Now,' he said, 'this is what you must remember. If ever you see an old French table with the linings of the drawers in mahogany, such a table was usually made for the Kings of France.' And he said to me, 'Don't you ever forget that because one day that'll be very useful to you.'

Well, years go by, nearly thirty-five years later, about eight years ago, I'm called into a house just below Monmouth. I walk through this large house, very nice pieces of furniture, porcelain, glass, everything of the finest, and eventually I get into a large garage. This garage had three very large bays and one bay was completely stacked with furniture, and I could just see, glinting at me out of this pile, another French table.

It was necessary to get it out to start with because it was actually tied up with a waggon rope. There was a thick rope round the middle holding in what looked likely to be a drawer. I said to the fellow, 'Fetch that table out.' So he fetched it out and together we took this rope off and the

[1] Roger Vandercruse called Lacroix, 1728–99.

drawer flew out. It was a drawer that was held by a hidden spring which had obviously broken, so that when you pushed the drawer in, there was nothing to retain it and the spring operated and just threw the drawer back at you as soon as you took your hand off it. The drawer flew out, I picked it up and of course, to my absolute amazement, it was mahogany-lined. I turned it up, it was beautifully signed by Oeben[1], a most eminent *Maître Ébéniste,* who was cabinet-maker to Louis XV. Eventually this table was sold in Christie's for thirty-four thousand guineas.

You see, this is how you store knowledge. Thousands of drawers and tables I've pulled out, never did I find one that was mahogany-lined but this one. This might still be possible perhaps, although I think as the years go by the opportunities for finding something like this will occur much less frequently. But this could possibly happen with a book, a piece of china, or some such article. As a matter of fact in the very selfsame house I really found something. I find it difficult to satisfy my own mind that I found the French table. It must have been known in the family that it existed. But I really think that I did find a book.

It happened like this. Their silver had been deposited in a bank and it fell to me to have all the crates and boxes brought out of the bank into this house to inspect them. And amongst all this silver was a deal box, a champagne case it was actually, the top of which was absolutely rotten. I just tore it off, it wanted no breaking, and inside were some sodden pieces of newspaper that were round a few mediocre books. They were absolutely mouldy and useless. But as these very damp things were removed, the lower one got in the box the drier became the articles, and the very last thing of all was a thick book wrapped in paper which, when it was taken from the paper, was actually as clean as new. It was a Book of Hours, that is one of those Latin transcriptions of the Bible done by monks, several monks' life-work beautifully illuminated with full-page illustrations, all in vegetable colourings, the colours of course got from their gardens. And this was a book that was completed in about 1450 and it actually sold for thirty thousand guineas.

But of all things I might say I've found I feel quite confident that I really found this book. I don't think the family had any idea at all that they

[1] François Oeben, 1720–63.

possessed such a valuable volume, and of course those of you who never experience anything like this can't appreciate to the full the terrific satisfaction one gets out of finding such a thing as this, and of course bringing it to some successful end. The hours and hours and hours that one gives in turning out old cupboards, old houses, old cellars, old attics to find nothing are made up for by the joy and the satisfaction one reaps when you find something of this nature—it's most satisfying. Of course, this is actually what I'm employed to do, what I've enjoyed doing all my life, and the very fact that one has these successes, if that's the right word, is in itself most gratifying.

63 Sheraton sofa-table, c.1790

64 Georgian sofa-table, *c*.1800

And so to *63*—a sofa-table. There you see clearly illustrated the flaps on the short sides, two drawers on the one side and a similar arrangement on the other but dummies, obviously the blind side of the table standing against a sofa. That's a typical sofa-table of about 1790. You see how again nice clear-cut lines show off the Chinese famille rose vases. Same idea as with the Pembroke table. Just a plain satinwood border around the top, nice square end-standard supports.

Now these end-standards change about. You get them square-cut like that, you also get them turned. You notice the square stretcher on this earlier table, a square rail running, as in the photograph, high up under the drawers. On later tables the rail is turned and of course, as you well know, the sofa-tables do get up on nasty pillars eventually.

The end-standards, of course, are the square pillars at either end of the table, from which shoot out those splayed legs, and those splayed legs will date a table pretty well. For example, look at *63*. There you will see a square end-standard with the legs coming, as is said in the trade, straight off the column. The square end-standard goes straight into the sweep of the leg. This is the earliest type of leg of this nature and comes from a table

65 Regency sofa-table, c.1820

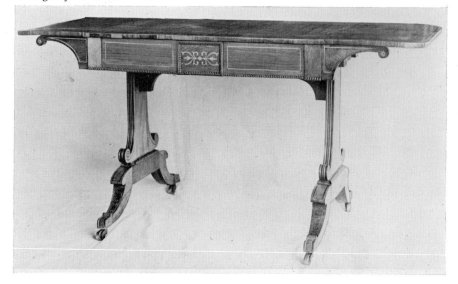

somewhere round about 1790. Now compare this with *64*. You have a similar square end-standard support with similar shaped legs coming off it. But these tend to have a bump where the leg joins the square end-standard. It's not particularly emphasised but nevertheless the leg comes up and over instead of going straight up to the column, as in *63*.

This is a sort of transition period from *63* to *65*, because here again you virtually have the same style of square end-standard. It is certainly shaped but it is those splay feet that one needs to consider. Here they are again, one each side of the end-standard, but *65* has some most pronounced bumps on it, virtually suffering acutely from toothache, and it would date way on to 1820–30. I don't suppose there are any sofa-tables before 1780 because these get their name by their affinity to sofas. They did actually stand at the backs of sofas – not high-back settees that were in use in the latter part of the Seventeenth and earlier Eighteenth centuries but low-back sofas which came in quite late, not before about 1780. So you see that *63* is possibly one of the earliest sofa-tables one would find.

It is curious how sofa-tables as such changed also in appearance. Now this one in *66* was actually shown in *Going for a Song*. This is pure Regency and everything that shows up light in that photograph is gilt metal. You see it's on a late pillar and a sort of flat base and quadruple supports.

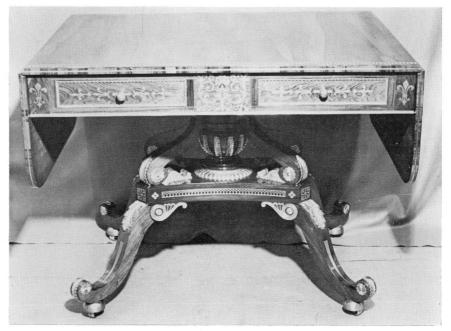

66 Regency sofa-table, c.1815

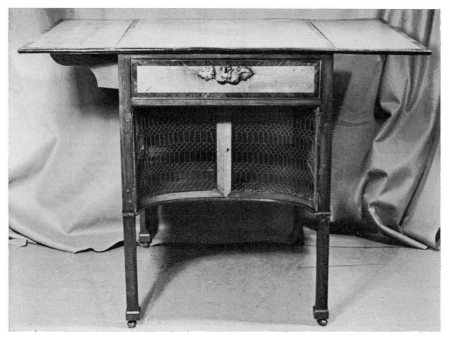

67 Chippendale breakfast-table, c.1795

It is quite typical of this period. You see the acanthus, the little scrolls under the legs, and all this, all in brass. Really very, very, very fussy. The drawer fronts, the inlaid frieze, the border all round the top. And on top there is an inlaid oval in the centre of the table, almost all brass. A table which can truthfully be described as very lively. But also very, very interesting because the condition of this table, the condition of the brass-work, in fact everthing about it, was absolutely superb. And I think without doubt it's one of the nicest later period sofa-tables that I have ever seen. The wood, of course, was rosewood.

67 shows a mahogany breakfast-table, photographed to show the concave doors with the brass wire grilles. Without the wire work (which goes down the sides of the table as well) and the doors, you simply have a two-flap Pembroke table. So you see, you really have a special kind of table in use

138

for breakfast. I believe the first table of this kind was attributed to Thomas Chippendale and had the same outline as the one in the photograph except that the doors were of pierced mahogany fretwork as were the sides. The idea behind these tables was apparently that, when the meal was over, the various foods, sauces, etc. were put underneath on the shelf and the two doors closed. Of course the fretwork and the brass wire grilles allowed air to circulate to keep the food fresh. It would, I think, date from about 1790–1800.

You will remember the Hepplewhite dressing-table (55). Here is one (68) made a little later when the fashion tends to change somewhat. In the first enclosed table the whole of the top lifts up and over, but in this one the top opens sideways. One half opens to the left, the other half to the right,

69 Sheraton knee-hole dressing-table, c.1790

revealing a fitted interior, again with a central mirror. This is very straight-forward, pure Sheraton with a nice clean line. Once more, you see the square taper legs, the bands of satinwood all much the same.

These enclosed dressing-tables have a mirror fitted in them. But fashion changes and you do come on to a type of table which is very desirable today, but which has no mirror attached to it at all, as we show in 69, a bow-front knee-hole dressing-table. Instead a swing toilet-mirror, a separate piece of furniture, stands on top of the dressing-table.

Notice the nice grain, all picked curls. I think it's true to say that when one sees the grain of the veneer going up the fronts of chests-of-drawers or tables this invariably is much nicer quality than grain which runs across the drawer fronts. Here's one with picked curls running up, just the same sort of thing as 78 (p. 158), just the same date. No inlay on this but the same square taper legs.

And you notice that this table is up on four legs, which means it's a dressing-table, whereas 70 shows a similar sort of table up on six legs and of course this is a sideboard. That's the great difference between knee-hole

70 Sheraton sideboard, c.1795

tables and sideboards, which have four legs at the front, two at the back. Often this is the only way of telling them apart: they might be exactly the same width, but the sideboard always stands on six legs whereas to my mind knee-hole dressing-tables stand on four legs only and are always bedroom pieces.

A knee-hole dressing-table usually has one long and two short deep drawers. It can also have two long and four short shallow drawers. It has a sort of an arched centre, which is why it's called a knee-hole; but it's impossible for anybody to sit at a small one and get their knees under. But it's a pretty shape. There's a great deal of difference, to my mind, between a knee-hole table and a knee-hole desk. People seem mystified by this but it seems so clear to me that a table must be up on legs. Anything that goes right down to the ground with drawers becomes, in my opinion, a desk. Whereas a table can have any number of drawers, on both sides, like double-sided writing-tables, but at least it would be raised on legs.

Here again you see the same Eighteenth-century feature, these square taper legs (though the sideboard has spade feet) and there is just the same influence all the way through 70, the cross-banding with satinwood, the inlay with an oval white line or a round white line. This outline is so distinctive of the Eighteenth century. And again the six legs of sideboards change as they get later in period. Just like Pembroke tables, just like sofa-tables, that degenerate, to my way of thinking, to having central pillars ornamented with many collars, becoming heavier and clumsier as they get up to say 1840. It's just the same with a sideboard. It starts off in the late Eighteenth century with a fine round turned leg. This turned leg, to my mind, corresponds to the central pillar. Six turned legs which get heavier, more clumsy, more fussy and more ugly as they develop through the next fifty years. So one can practically date a sideboard from the detail of the leg on which it stands, particularly if that leg happens to be turned.

It's a curious thing, in a way that a Baptist minister called Thomas Sheraton should give his name so much to sideboards but you see, there were no sideboards before about 1790 and Sheraton saw the possibility of uniting Robert Adam's side-tables with their pair of cupboards that stand to either side with urns on the top. Sheraton compressed these three things together, providing cellarettes in the deep drawers to either side, which more or less corresponded to the cupboards, and a centre-piece with a long

71 Sheraton half-round sideboard, c.1790

drawer representing the side-table. The three pieces were put together on paper by Thomas Sheraton and he was the first man to introduce this word 'sideboard'.

This was no doubt extremely convenient to people who lived in smaller homes, because normally a small Adam side-table, flanked by these urns, would occupy anything up to eight feet; whereas Sheraton sideboards (a biggish one is say six foot six, and a small one is right down to four feet) today have so much come back into favour with people living in small flats in town.

You see 71 is another sideboard. You notice this differs from all the others in that it is a complete half-round. These half-round sideboards are scarcer than those made in the normal form and they've got extra drawers, though obviously some of the drawers taper very much to a point, because they can't all run back the full depth of the sideboard. But you see it's still on six legs and still has something of a knee-hole underneath the centre shallower drawer. Not always does one find a knee-hole there. You see that's really just been ornamented with those satinwood corner pieces which in this instance are called 'spandrels', not brackets. They look just the same as the brass spandrels one sees on the corners of clock dials. Not always is there a knee-hole or this recess under the shallow drawer, on occasions there's another drawer, so there could be two drawers in the centre. This bottom drawer you would usually call a napery drawer, obviously where the linen was kept.

Chests

The oldest piece of furniture in England is what is commonly known as a chest, or coffer, call it what you will. These are virtually boxes, formed by slabs of wood pegged together, with solid front, back and ends, and a solid top. This was the very first type of hold-all that was created, mainly for linen, but it sometimes had loose boxes lying about inside, in which there might have been needlework or jewellery.

If you visit a house in Derbyshire, Haddon Hall, for example, in the kitchen there is a kind of chest which is really no more than the trunk of a tree, just a crudely shaped square. You can envisage the actual trunk with the middle of it gouged out, as it were, and there it stands. It is a salting trough because there's a hole bored through the base, and I suppose it's one of the earliest and certainly crudest bits of furniture. But from this type of thing sprang all these chests. They were profusely carved, often with designs from old books or old missals, mainly depicting scenes from the Bible or from early biblical works.

72 shows an early Gothic front. You get them like this carved with bust portraits in roundels, very early, very nice. There you see a very plain, probably Sixteenth-century chest, with just those three busts carved within those roundels and a bit of leafage underneath – probably Flemish this, but early, crude to look at, and a good example of the solid wood just pegged together by a joiner.

144

72 16th-century chest, *c*.1550

73 17th-century Nonsuch chest, *c*.1680

And then they took on different designs in the front, and when one gets along to the end of the Sixteenth century there is a type of chest that has a certain amount of history behind it, in that it's inlaid in a parquet design of what looks like some Eastern palace (*73*). These are always attributed to a palace built by Henry VIII called the Nonsuch Palace near Cheam in Surrey, which was later completely destroyed by fire. This type of chest has panels illustrating in marquetry the façades of the Palace, and so these go under this name of Nonsuch chests.

Other chests, of course, are much more ordinary pieces of furniture – plain, panelled, fronts only panelled, the panels perhaps carved with linen-fold – you'll recall this nice type of perpendicular carving, representing the vertical folds in a linen sheet. Linen-fold panelled chests – with all sorts of

145

differently shaped (though usually rectangular) panels, carved, inlaid, done all sorts of ways – with tiny ones made in Wales called Love Chests. You know how these people when they fell in love seemed either to want to make a chest to give to their betrothed, or to sit and carve some spoons – Welsh love spoons – peculiar to Wales, as are these tiny little chests called Welsh Love Chests.

Of course the same motif one finds on all these chests is that round flower-head called a Tudor rose. It's curious too, I suppose, that there are so many of these still in existence, but it's because they were made in English oak which didn't suffer through getting wet. One must remember these things stood on stone floors; they just stood on rushes that would be swilled down, so probably they stood in damp. But this oak seems to have survived this, because there are many good chests still about, and I suppose the old question of supply and demand comes in. To my mind a chest made between perhaps 1660 and 1700 and onwards seems very low in price when one knows quite well that it can be bought for as little as £20 or £30.

It's a curious thing how these values are expressed. A thing made in 1660 isn't necessarily worth two or three times what a piece of furniture made in say 1760 might be worth. Generally speaking, chests are comparatively plentiful and this is why their price is relatively low. Of course, it is also true that there's always been this curious lack of interest in oak – probably because it is in appearance rather heavy, rather sombre, very dark and not so well made. People all the time like their homes brightened up rather than dulled down by pieces of oak furniture. I think this is shown most particularly when one pays a visit to the Victoria and Albert.

The Museum is so arranged that you can see period rooms furnished as they were. They start from way back in the Seventeenth century, then gradually are succeeded one room by another, tracing the history of our homes through the lovely figured walnut furniture of Queen Anne into the Eighteenth century, up through William Kent, through Thomas Chippendale to George Hepplewhite, Robert Adam and Thomas Sheraton. You can look over your shoulder, as it were, and see behind you the early room furnished in oak. You can compare it to the room a hundred or so years later, and just see the difference in style and the reason why people these days generally prefer to live with mahogany and the lighter type of furniture than with this early but rather heavy English oak.

Another reason why there are still so many of these chests is that they were very strongly made – by joiners – and, of course, being the kind of article they are, they don't get moved about and so have much less wear and tear. As these chests come up to the end of the Seventeenth century, they tend to be put up on longer legs and occasionally have a drawer, or two small drawers, below, and then by natural progression the thing does become a chest-of-drawers. This, as everyone knows, is just an assemblage of open boxes, which slide in and out in a square carcase. These drawers – they're really nothing more nor less than sliding boxes. And again they were made all through the ages, right the way from early days.

The earliest type of chest-of-drawers, a Jacobean one, say, from the middle of the Seventeenth century, would usually be enclosed by outer doors. There's perhaps one long drawer, and then underneath a pair of cupboard doors which would enclose probably two long and two short, or three long and two short narrow drawers, and I suppose this is the first type of chest-of-drawers.

These chests-of-drawers are decorated with the same motifs as the coffer-chests, the cupboard doors resembling the carved panels in the coffer. They're either moulded, made up with shaped mouldings, or the doors can be inlaid with marquetry in holly and bog oak with all sorts of designs – Tudor roses, perhaps a bit more of the Nonsuch Palace, but all amounting to much the same thing in this new form, the chest-of-drawers. Very soon – round about 1670 – the cupboard doors are taken off, and you get a proper chest-of-drawers in the form that we know it now, either four long drawers, or three long and two short, or four long and two short – a chest-of-drawers.

To begin with, the drawer fronts themselves had the typical raised or sunk Jacobean panels, which tended to imitate the carved panels of coffers, not perhaps carved so much as inlaid with floral marquetry, or panelled out in those geometrical designs with the edges of the chest ornamented with what we call split balusters. They are the turned wooden pendants which are actually stuck on the front of these things just to give some added decoration.

One might wonder how they were produced. It was done quite easily by two pieces of wood being stuck together with a piece of paper in between, then put into a foot lathe, which was operated and the thing was turned. Once the piece has been turned to look like a round baluster out of a staircase rail, obviously a hot knife pressed through the joint will separate the paper and there you have your split baluster, both halves exactly matching but with a flat surface on the one side, so that it can be easily stuck onto the chest.

These chests are rather large, they're usually split into two halves, and this is useful, perhaps, in getting them upstairs today. Some of them are extremely nice, the mitring of the mouldings which form the raised panels being very deep, very shapey, all to geometrical designs. A good deal of work and labour went into these chests and yet, because they are big, perhaps because they're still in oak and dark, they don't bring the money that one would associate with a piece of furniture made in say 1670. They're not liked so much as the later chests, which I must say take on a much more shapey form, and to my mind are much more attractive.

But maybe one reason why people don't like these early oak chests is because the drawers are as it were suspended on what are known as side runners instead of sliding *on* the runners as the Eighteenth-century ones are. Well, obviously if a drawer has been pulled in and out for some two or three hundred years, this has worn to some extent, and often the deep drawers in these old chests are not all that easy to pull out. Of course a good repair could put this right. Still, by and large, when you remember that they are three hundred years old, it is curious how you can buy a chest of this nature for a certain sum of money, but a chest made one hundred years later could make as much as six or seven times the price that the older but cruder chest would bring.

Of course it's perhaps also because this wood is actually dark, there is no real life in it, it doesn't exude a fine colour. When one stops to think it makes one realise what these homes must have been like in about 1660. All this heavy black oak in rooms that had dark oak panelling, small mullion windows. They really must have been most depressing when there was virtually no light to enhance the furniture, nor any furniture which took on a different form, because after all's said and done, the early oak chests-of-drawers do no more than copy the plain or carved oak panelling which was already on the walls.

Of course with the introduction of walnut, in the William and Mary period, say from 1690 and for the next thirty years, you get what were, I

148

74 Adam cabinet,
c.1785

suppose, some of the prettiest chests-of-drawers that were ever made – made in figured walnut and of supreme workmanship. During this period sometimes the chests-of-drawers were popped up on stands, and this undoubtedly gave birth, later on in the Eighteenth century, to tallboys, which are just double chests, a chest-of-drawers standing upon another chest-of-drawers. But round about this period we're now discussing, Queen Anne, the chests went up on six-legged stands, with pretty stretchers. Again there was plenty of floral marquetry used – English marquetry, so very different to Dutch.

The difference does seem to mystify some people, and yet to my mind there is a tremendous difference. The English marquetry is finer. Now I know that's a peculiar word to use in this context. Let me explain. You get a bouquet of flowers, inlaid in marquetry on the top of a chest-of-drawers. It is the composition of the marquetry that is finer in English furniture than in Dutch. By that I mean the flower-head would probably be made of 6, or 8 or 9 pieces of wood, whereas in Dutch marquetry the flower-head would be made of one or two pieces of wood and no more – much coarser. This perhaps is a better word.

One can recognise English cabinet work at its finest by looking at 74. This has been deliberately photographed so that all the front and a certain amount of the top can be seen. Made in satinwood – I think the feathering of the grain shows this as satinwood – it shows the inlaid floral frieze above the two doors with the inlaid canted corners to either side. The doors have a bouquet of English flowers tied with a ribbon, inlaid into the satinwood. These flowers, collectively and individually, look exactly like real flowers but they are in fact different coloured pieces of wood cut into the blossom and foliage shapes, and let into other pieces of wood. The skill is that the cabinet-maker has given life to the wood, so that the bouquets actually look alive and real. One can also just discern a fine inlaid oval in the top within a floral wreath, and one should notice the shaped ends – shaped serpentine ends instead of straight ends – thereby giving more shape to the canted corners.

Such commodes were made to the neo-classic designs of Robert Adam by Thomas Chippendale, by George Hepplewhite in the French taste, and of course by a great number of other eminent cabinet-makers whose names, alas, we do not know. It is only when documentary proof, such as a receipted account, is found that one can speak with authority of these other cabinet-makers, e.g. the fine commode by John Cobb at Corsham, Wilts, the home of Lord Methuen, and the work of Peter Langlois for the Duchess of Northumberland at Syon House, Middlesex. Actually, the commode shown in the photograph is one of a pair recently bequeathed to Cheltenham Museum and did occupy a prominent part in one of the *Going for a Song* programmes.

Then there is a style of marquetry, known as seaweed marquetry, which is so thin and fine, just like a mat of seaweed. This is so typically English, this cannot fail to be recognised. But generally speaking a panel of English marquetry put beside a similar panel of Dutch marquetry is easily distinguished by its much finer detail.

These chests-on-stands, of course, often stood on stone floors, which were swilled down. They're nearly always made in walnut, because this was the period when walnut was introduced. Walnut or other soft woods, like chestnut, but all really very soft, very susceptible to worm and rot, and invariably one finds the legs and stretchers replaced on most of these early chests-on-stands. It's not to be wondered at really. The feet would rot in the wet, perhaps a leg would get a bit wormy because, as I say, they're so susceptible to worm. Down would crash the chest and so all the legs would have to be renewed. It is really quite rare to find a chest with its original spiral or cabriole legs and the very pretty stretchers shaped in the William and Mary period to unite all the legs.

Round about 1700 we get a great vogue for lacquer – japanning, as it was called. It was a method of copying the lacquer which for some while had been brought into England from the Far East by the East India Company. A terrific lot of lacquered work was done during this late William and Mary and early Queen Anne period. It didn't last very long because I imagine that people wanted the new types of wood that were being used with such pretty figuring, all burrs.

One gets beautifully made chests-of-drawers all of similar form, three long and two short drawers, either veneered in walnut (not the normal straight-grain walnut, but walnut cut round the branches, or better still down in the roots of the trunk of the tree) or laburnum or olive, cut cross-wise so that you have what we call oyster shells, cut across the small branch of a tree and then shaped into hexagonal or octagonal panels.

Just think of the work involved. A chap with an octagonal piece of wood in his hand – and it's only three inches across – joins it with other similar pieces of wood, making absolutely true, correct, beautiful joints on at least eight sides, and so continues building it up, veneering as he goes, like a patchwork quilt, but actually doing a patchwork design in pieces of wood. These oyster-shell, as they're called, chests in walnut or laburnum, are sought for, and so are the peculiar little chests which were produced about this time.

These are always tiny, and this may be why they're liked. They're known as bachelor chests, and they are extremely rare, particularly so in walnut. 75, in mahogany, is a nice example. They're tiny, as I say, and what constitutes a bachelor chest is simply the same outline as a normal chest-of-drawers, perhaps three and two, or three and one narrow tiny drawer, *but it has a folding top*. A top, like a card-table's, unfolds outwards opening towards one like the flap of a bureau. There are two bearers just at the side of the top drawers which pull out and support this flap when it's opened, so that it turns itself into a chest-of-drawers with a nearly square table-top. Closed it's no more than about eighteen inches deep, if that, and usually about two feet six wide. A very pretty and very rare little chest. I don't really know why they're called bachelor chests, but I suppose the object of the thing was perhaps two-fold. One would infer that a man could press his clothes on the top, when it is opened, or even deal with any matters of correspondence.

The bachelor chest, as such, although it is found in mahogany, and so made until about 1740 perhaps, must have soon given way to a chest-of-drawers that was fitted with a slide. These slides are usually lined. They're invariably called writing slides, and that I think is quite wrong. They are nothing more nor less than brushing slides. It is very unusual to get a walnut chest with a shaped front. There are some walnut chests-of-drawers which are bow-fronted, and they carry a little slide usually above the drawers, and, like the bachelor chest, are always quite small, and really a most attractive size.

This was a period when things seemed to develop rather quickly, because, apart from chests-of-drawers as such, the innovation of a bachelor chest, the introduction of a brushing slide in a little tiny chest, the chest going up on stands, we get now the first sight of a tallboy. This is nothing more than one chest standing on another. Often the corners of the top are canted, usually fluted; sometimes the canted corners carry on down the bottom half as well. These are a little bit better, but there are others in walnut with beautifully figured fronts. Ordinary walnut from the trunk of a tree is a very insipid wood. It has got no figure. It's got just a poor straight grain, and really the trunk of a walnut tree is only used to cut into veneers for veneering ends of chests-of-drawers or tallboys, but lower down, amongst the roots, you get this wonderful figuring and the walnut tallboys of this age are beautifully veneered, on pine as a rule, sometimes on oak, but always with this pretty figured veneer. With the passing of some 200 years the colour has mellowed into what we call a golden honey. Some of the colours of these walnut pieces are absolutely superb.

There's a curious feature in these tallboys which adds money to them. It's a sort of sunray or a rising sun, which you can find on some pieces, and it's nearly always inlaid in the centre of the bottom drawer. This is called a sunburst. It's usually inlaid in ebony and holly and is a distinctive feature. And I suppose it was the first time that a motif like this was introduced onto a piece of furniture. This adds a considerable sum to any piece of walnut furniture on which it can be found, and it's usually on the earlier pieces. It's inclined to be William and Mary, but falls in the general category of all walnut of this period, between 1695 and 1715, something like that.

75 Bachelor chest, *c*.1740

As the century progresses, one gets the introduction of mahogany. I don't think there was much mahogany in this country prior to 1730, and it may well be that there was not much mahogany furniture about before 1740. Then it's all mahogany, this lovely Spanish mahogany coming in from Cuba. Really beautiful wood. Straighter in grain, of course, than the figured walnut, but so lovely to work, and now one gets little mahogany chests with slides, commonly known as Chippendale chests, of usually three or four long drawers with this same brushing slide over. And we get all sorts of shapes. You can get bow-fronted chests, concave

153

76 Chippendale knee-hole, c.1775

chests. A concave chest is an unusual piece of furniture, with the drawer fronts all curved inwards. There are not very many of those about. Then there are the serpentine chests – with a nice free-flowing in-and-out curve that suggests their name.

All these have degrees of rarity, and of course there are literally hundreds and hundreds of straight-front chests-of-drawers, oak-lined, well made, poorly made, country made. Nevertheless they all have the same type of outline fitted with either four or five drawers. But whatever the outline the mahogany used during the last half of the Eighteenth century and the workmanship that the cabinet-makers put into it are very fine. These cabinet-makers of this period used such care when they made this furniture. And the cleanliness of it! By cleanliness I mean with regard to glue. No glue anywhere. Everything washed off inside and out. I suppose the scarcest chest in mahogany is one with a serpentine front. Running close to it would be a concave one, then a bow, and then a straight-front chest-of-drawers.

76 seems to me to be a modification of a straight-front chest-of-drawers.

Here you have what is known as a knee-hole. It has that recessed central cupboard with a surround – in this case of eight drawers. The little bit of shaped frieze above the recessed centre cupboard is in fact a drawer. So there are altogether eight drawers. But you see this is Chippendale, it has almost all the same features as the serpentine chest I shall be coming to very soon (77). Canted corners again, but these are reeded while the serpentine chest has applied fret decoration. Here you've got a nice little feature in the carved capitals, all carved in wood and gilt. This is one of those little things which again elevate this piece of furniture from what might have been called a more ordinary knee-hole. Again, referring to the brushing slides, here we have a slide above the top drawers. Just a pull-out solid slide in this case, and the ogee-shaped feet are a good example – as shows very clearly on the right-hand end foot. There is a hangover here, too, on this knee-hole from the William and Mary and Queen Anne periods, because there you have inlaid in ebony and satinwood a rather nice sunburst on the recessed central cupboard door. These sunbursts are sometimes recessed but always inlaid in this manner. And to my mind quite a nice feature on walnut and on this type of mahogany.

Another rather interesting thing on the knee-hole is the arrangement of the four feet in the front. This to my mind tends to make these little knee-holes very attractive. You realise this bracket-foot moulding, the ogee shape, has to be worked on a bench. That means to say that a piece of mahogany, say nine inches wide – that is the height of the foot – has to be of enough thickness for the cabinet-maker to work this moulding. This sort of in-and-out moulding, this ogee shape, has just the same outline as an ogee-shaped wineglass. It has to be worked on the bench and then the bracket foot cut after the moulding has been done. So there's quite a lot more work in a rather pretty ogee-shaped foot.

As to these slides I think without question that, when they occur in pieces of furniture which might be deemed upstairs pieces of furniture – such as chests-of-drawers and tallboys and wardrobes (you occasionally get a slide in a wardrobe), they were certainly for brushing and not for writing. Now when we get downstairs furniture like this knee-hole desk (76), then the slide must be for writing because, although there is a little knee-hole, it is too low and too shallow for anyone to sit up to it in order to write upon its top.

I'm quite sure that this knee-hole was a piece of furniture constructed solely for use downstairs, but there's no reason at all why it couldn't be taken up. In fact one finds a lot of knee-holes upstairs in bedrooms in use as dressing-tables, because they do provide a good-sized top, quite deep from front to back, which allows ladies plenty of room for a mirror and for their cosmetics.

77 Chippendale serpentine-front chest, c.1770

77 shows another chest-of-drawers, not with the more common straight front but with a serpentine shape. You notice the rather nice grain in the front. This denotes good quality, and with such chests-of-drawers they are always better if the top drawer is fitted. This means to say it has a green baize-lined slide within the drawer, which can be pushed back when the drawer is opened to reveal an adjustable mirror and an arrangement of small, wooden compartments and covers, all fixed within the drawer to hold jewellery, razors, pins, all sorts of things of that nature.

Now 77 has that fitted top drawer with the three long drawers below and it has canted corners. These are the corners which stand on the skew as you can see in the illustration. Again, the use of applied fret down them, and the chest takes on a little more importance when the ends are shaped. This has what we call shaped ends, because each end of the chest comes forward in a straight line but then bends outward to join that canted corner. Of course, it has the usual moulded bracket feet and a rather nice set of English rococo gilt handles.

78 shows a bow-front chest. The point about this chest is simply that the cabinet-maker here has been to a lot of trouble to pick two sheets of veneer, and as it were, lay the chest-of-drawers upon its back before using the veneer. He then matched up the two sheets so that they carry right up continuously through all the drawers, in fact the whole of the front of the chest. This method of veneering is one I appreciate very much indeed, because here is a cabinet-maker going to a little more trouble. Curiously enough, pieces of furniture which are veneered up the front always seem to be very much better quality than those that might be veneered across. This chest has what we know as a splay foot, a style of foot – particularly when it's graceful and with a frieze running round like this – that allows one to say that this is Hepplewhite and dated about 1780-90.

Notice it has a slide above the top drawer, a little, one-inch thick, green baize-lined slide, which is often called a writing slide, but which in point of fact, as I've said, was a brushing slide. This, of course, is coming down the scale. Although it's attractive and nice, this is worth nothing like the value of the serpentine chest with the canted corners (77). And then of course we come to straight-front chests-of-drawers. There seems to be no need to illustrate any of these. They are so well known. Here again those which are veneered up the fronts of the chest, all over the front drawers,

78 Hepplewhite bow-front chest, c.1790

are usually very nice quality. And, of course, straight-front chests-of-drawers also have brushing slides.

Of course the turned wooden knob-handles on the Hepplewhite bow-front chest (78) are relatively modern. Here we have lost the original brass handles. Possibly an odd one came off, but more likely the whole lot were stripped off during Victorian times for some reason or the other. You see how attractive the knee-hole (76) looks, with the original rococo handles and those rather pretty C-scroll shaped key-hole escutcheons. To my mind it makes the piece of furniture look so much better.

Once again, just as with the walnut period, so with the mahogany, you get tallboys. More double chests, one chest on another, straight-fronted like they were in walnut times, bow-fronted, and even better ones with serpentine fronts. And on some of these tallboys the cabinet-makers have really gone to town; canted corners may be profusely carved, the mouldings all carved with nice acanthus, or other flower-head type of decoration. The ogee-shaped feet perhaps carved again, smothered in carving. The bottom moulded with maybe gadroons, all going to produce just a better type of article. And, of course, the handles come into this a good deal. Really fine English gilt metal handles.

Talking of tallboys it's a curious thing that during our married life for at least 41 years we have always wanted and have never yet bought a tallboy. I always promised I would buy a good tallboy when I saw one. About six or seven years ago I went home and told my wife I should be buying a tallboy, because at last I'd seen in a sale a tallboy I liked. Superb quality, with a wonderful set of English rococo handles. A good article. It was one of the sales conducted by my firm and on the view day I was there when a lady came up to me and said, 'Tell me something about that tallboy.' And I told her quite truthfully it was the nicest tallboy I'd ever seen, and that the handles, everything about it, were absolutely original. So she turned round and she said, 'Well then, if you say that, you buy it for me.' I said, 'Buy it?' 'Yes, you just buy it. I shan't mind what it costs. Buy it.' So this is the reason why we are still looking for a tallboy.

Curiously enough the present owner of the tallboy is quite friendly with us, and we have on occasions visited her home. The last time she very kindly gave us dinner, and it was then that I told her this story. And of course we were allowed to go through into another room and have a peep at our tallboy – because I still call it mine, although it reposes in another person's home.

Bureaux and bureau-bookcases

I suppose everyone knows exactly what a bureau is, with its sloping front that opens to reveal some sort of fitted interior of small drawers and pigeon-holes. Of course it has long drawers below, and in the early Eighteenth century and even in the late Seventeenth century many bureaux were made carrying bookcase tops. So here we have, in 79, a walnut bureau-bookcase – nicely figured as you see. Made in English walnut – all this wood cut quite low down in the roots or against the branches in order to get this nice figure.

I feel that this bureau-bookcase we're looking at originally had mirror doors. One might say they nearly always had mirror doors and I'm certain this one did with, of course, the usual raw silvered back. The opening and shutting of the doors often caused slight movement of the back-board that might be holding the mirrors in, so that it actually scratched or rubbed against the raw silver and, over the course of time, the plates became so worn that one could hardly see an image in them. Hence you often find they've been taken away and either replaced by new mirrors, which one can nearly always tell because of their brilliance, or by clear glass in order that one can see the books or the ornaments displayed behind.

79 (opposite) George I bureau-bookcase, c.1720

Why I feel this one for certain had mirror doors is because you notice under the centre of both doors there is a little shiny round mark. This is a tiny brass knob which, when pulled, brings out a little slide. These are known as candle slides and, when they were pulled out, one rested a lighted candle upon them in order to gain extra reflection from the mirrors above and throw the light as it were down into the bureau, so that the writer could the better see what he or she was doing. But there it is—a normal type of Queen Anne or George I walnut bureau-bookcase.

80 shows a very good bureau-bookcase. These all take the same sort of outline—the normal bureau base, the bookcase top, sometimes with solid panel doors like this one, at other times with mirror panels. You notice the swan-neck cornice and those very large dentils carved with flower-heads and that bird in the middle. I don't know what that is, but I suppose it might be a dove. Then you have the applied fret frieze – you see all these things have parallels. You remember the applied fret frieze down the

81 The bureau-bookcase in 80 with the flap open

legs of the Chippendale dining-chair (21), well this is round about the same time, the middle of the Eighteenth century. And you see that this book-case is fitted with shelves and small drawers inside, but has the edges to the panels rather nicely carved with acanthus, and this carving is repeated in a similar way around the base of the top of the bureau. Inside the flap (81) there is a central cupboard door, secret drawers behind the pillars, the other usual small drawers and pigeon-holes. And there's that carved moulding, absolutely tying the top to the bottom.

And you'll notice the bureau has four long drawers below and again the bottom moulding is decorated with that rather nice acanthus sort of carving. Very reminiscent of gilt gesso work this, because you know gesso has a base of carved wood. It gets its name gesso from the preparation which is put upon the carved wood in order that the gold leaf will the better adhere to it, for it won't stick on wood. The secret drawers in this bookcase are, I'm afraid, not so secret these days. They're nearly all exactly like that, covered by the fluted pillars, and they pull right out. Notice the lovely unstained wainscot oak with which it is framed together

– no attempt to make it look old, absolutely left as brand-new, and of course it's got age, simply because the thing has been made and in use for well over 200 years.

In a similar way, one can take one of the small drawers from inside the bookcase top (*82*) and this clearly shows the manner of construction. Lovely wainscot oak with the red walnut front. Though you can't see the dovetail, it's obvious it has never moved, and again no attempt to make the thing look old. You see, this is the great thing with identifying old pieces of furniture; if a man made a drawer like this today, the oak would look different. This oak looks brownish, and the modern oak today would

83 Underside of drawer

look white. He would have to stain and mess about with the inside to try and give it the age which this genuinely possesses. If people would only learn to recognise this point – that there's been no attempt at all to make it look old. Underneath this drawer are some grooves (83) caused by it running in over something like a paperclip or a screwhead for a number of years. The oak has literally been scraped away in a place or two – but there's no difference whatever in the colour because the wood itself never had any stain.

This bureau-bookcase (80) is in that somewhat mysterious wood called red walnut. I know many people have written to me and I've been asked to settle all sorts of differences over what is red walnut. Well, mahogany didn't come into England in any quantity before about 1730, but the English walnut in the straight-grain trunk is such an insipid wood – it really only becomes beautiful when it is cut low down in the root and possesses that wonderful burr grain, that this red walnut, as it's called, was imported from France and Italy. It is referred to in many reference books as French walnut or Grenoble walnut, much prized by cabinet-makers. The severe winter of 1709 destroyed much of the walnut in Central Europe and its export to England was prohibited in 1720. Incidentally, another walnut was then imported to take its place – from Virginia – and this has much darker markings in the grain, being sometimes called black walnut. But red walnut is a lovely wood to use, as you can see from the grain in the panels of the door, and if you could actually handle this, you would realise that it is very like mahogany.

As you know I've so often talked about drawers and the way the grain goes in the bottom board–that when it runs lengthways the piece is before 1730, when crossways after 1730. Of course this is only a rough guide and there must be exceptions. The grain on the drawers of 80 dates it at about 1730, and yet I feel it must be a little later. There is much about it that suggests William Kent – the very large 'tooth-like' dentils around the cornice, the egg and tongue moulding immediately below these big dentils, and yet the fretwork frieze suggests a Chippendale type of frieze, so I would date this one about 1740. Of course the feet would be a Nineteenth-century renewal and the pierced brass plate handles are of a little later type than the date I have ascribed to the bureau-bookcase (see p.213).

Many pieces of furniture which are in two halves have at some time or

85 Chippendale wardrobe, c.1765

other been separated, and old pieces have come to be married together. Now everything in *80* ties up exactly, the grain of the drawers, the carved mouldings, the colour of the wood, the style and balance – everything just ties this top to this bottom. But if the piece had the carved mouldings round the bookcase panels and also round the top edge of the bureau, and then we suddenly found the bureau below had a very pretty black or white line, or a piece of cable-stringing, then any change like that between the two halves simply means that a marriage has taken place.

When one examines a chest-on-stand, a tallboy, a bureau-bookcase, a cabinet, a china cabinet-on-stand, if on the one part there is a narrow black line of stringing introduced, there should be just that same black line of stringing introduced onto the other. Not black in one part and white in another. If it is an eighth of an inch thick on the top, it will be an eighth of an inch thick on the base and any difference in thicknesses, widths or designs of stringing shows that the top really bears no relation to the base, although both might be old.

84 shows another bureau-bookcase. This one hasn't by any means the amount of work on it that *80* has. You see much the same sort of thing, solid panelled doors, not with carved mouldings this time, just an astragal with broken corners. An architectural cornice, not a swan-neck – little dentils and a bureau base below, quite plain, quite genuine, original handles with ogee feet. Very similar in outline to *80* but so different in the cost of production.

And you see how you can get these bureau-bookcases with a tremendous lot of work on them, or plainer like this one, and you can get exactly the same idea shown in *85*, which in point of fact is a wardrobe. Instead of having the bureau base below, in the wardrobe you have just two long and two short drawers. But otherwise it's practically identical. Here again, a little more work. You notice the quality of the veneers, all the picked curls used on both pieces of furniture (*84* and *85*) but here you see a little extra detail in the moulding around the top of the base, gadrooning, just so the top settles in rather prettily, and again we've got a more elaborate swan-neck cornice, this time with a pierced fret in between and rather large dentils all the way around.

To me one seems so much related to the other, and of course there is yet a third slight variation (*86*). Here again you have another bookcase – a secretaire-bookcase. This is almost the same as the bureau-bookcase (*84*), just serves the same purpose but has a glazed top part, the main difference being that there's no sloping fall-front flap enclosing drawers. In fact the top drawer has a fall-front. This drawer front pulls out about six or eight inches and is then stopped by the arrangement of wedges underneath. By pressing on two catches, you drop the front down and you find inside that it's green baize-lined and again has the fitting of small drawers and pigeon-holes. So there you have bureau-bookcases and their cousins, the secretaire-bookcase and the wardrobe, all Eighteenth-century, all very similar, some with solid panel doors, some with glazed doors, but all very closely related.

I would imagine *84* could be dated round about 1750-60; you see, you have this rather stiff architectural cornice. One always associates architectural designs with our old friend William Kent. This isn't a Kent piece of furniture but there is that rather stiff architectural cornice above, so it's probably a transitional piece. Now the date of *85* is later. This is Chippendale, about 1760-70, rather pretty. You see you have this fret. This fret keeps appearing all over the place, under the brackets of chairs, down the sides of canted corners, up in the cornices, as with this wardrobe.

The secretaire-bookcase would be even later but still the influence of Chippendale is to be seen. You see, if you look at *84* and *85* together, you'll notice that the solid panel doors have an astragal bead around them, forming a panel with what is known as broken corners. You'll notice just the same effect around the drawer of the secretaire in the secretaire-bookcase (*86*). Again, a raised astragal applied onto the drawer front, with the broken corners to give a nice effect; but you see, you also have this sort of Gothic design to the glazing of the bar doors. Sort of a church window effect, and this would be coming up to about 1780.

It must be remembered that all these men – Adam, Hepplewhite, Sheraton – were influenced by Chippendale's designs and none of them are very far removed from the originals, although Chippendale's would be much more ornate. *85* to me is unmistakably Chippendale, with its pierced fret, the rather pretty swan-neck cornice, the astragal with the broken corners and that gadroon border carved around the middle.

Although there is this great similarity between these three pieces and all really have their origins in the rather more ornate illustrations in Chippendale's *Director*, here again you notice this process of development,

170

87 Queen Anne bureau, in mulberry, c.1705

of supplying furniture more for a new middle class which is appearing in England. It's no longer the tremendously ornate and very costly furniture such as Chippendale designed for mansions, but, although with the same outline, much more staid to suit the purses of this new class. Of course there were many simple bureaux made. They had no bookcase tops, and on some occasions a wonderful effect was achieved by using different woods in order to veneer the exterior of a bureau, such as the one shown in *87* which is in mulberry. They're marvellous things, bureaux, absolutely marvellous things. As long as you can get the flap closed and lock it. Oh,

172

what a whole heap of miscellanea it does contain underneath! No need to tidy it up. Just a complete mess like a good waste-paper basket.

But look at the effect of using a wood which is a tremendous favourite of mine, mulberry. You can never mistake that. There's a really remarkable bureau, made in about 1700 to 1710, and veneered all over in mulberry. It's just like tortoise-shell, but a lovely sort of honey colour – most attractive. Incidentally this was a bureau which did appear in one of our country

88 George II bureau on legs, *c.*1750

house sales and, I suppose because it was in this rare wood, it brought the rather high price of 1,000 guineas about 15 years ago.

Another type of bureau is shown in *88*. Here you have a George II mahogany bureau, raised up on cabriole legs at the front, with square heavy legs, slightly lightened by a chamfer, at the back. Although this has nice simple lines it's not good quality, for the shell which rests in the centre of the frieze of the stand is not crisply carved – it's too flat. This type of shell, flat as it looks, because it really has not much life, is sometimes a pointer to furniture made in Ireland. You can also see the same flat effect on the leg. It's a cabriole leg, of course, with the same outline and ball-and-claw foot, but you see the claws are a bit skimpy. They do not really clench the ball. They rather stretch over the ball, and there is this difference. A good English claw-and-ball foot really shows, to my mind, the straining claws outstretched and completely encircling the ball.

Here is a secretaire-chest, a very simple outline (*89*). But I can sort of hear the cabinet-maker in about 1780 saying to himself, 'Oh well, that's a jolly nice chest down the road, but I'm going to make a chest now that will make everyone's hair stand on end.' And he kept himself to just the same outline, but he produced a chest like this – the two top drawers being actually one, with a simulated front. All the panels are in burr yew. This is a lovely wood, full of figure, just like burr walnut. In fact I think I like it better. It has satinwood cock-beads, it's crossbanded with rosewood, and it's about 1780. You can call it Hepplewhite because of the splay-shaped legs. It's superb for condition and workmanship.

Inside the secretaire's fitted drawer there are just three or four small drawers and pigeon-holes. The drawer sides are no more than a sixteenth to an eighth of an inch thick. Absolutely as brand-new but as firm as a rock. And the whole adds up to a most attractive thing. Still possessing just that simple outline and really nothing to it, except the superb woods that the cabinet-maker decided he would make it in.

One's mind now passes on from bureau-bookcases and secretaires to the type of thing shown in *90*. This is not actually a piece of furniture for writing on. It is a cabinet, although here again it has its exact counterpart which is known as an escritoire. Generally this type of furniture is in English walnut, figured walnut, and has that moulded cornice, with the mouldings always worked in cross-grain. The plain ovolo moulding is

89 Hepplewhite burr-yew secretaire-chest, *c.*1780

actually a long drawer that completely pulls out and is always referred to as a map drawer – it probably held maps or large portfolios.

Unlike this cabinet, an escritoire for writing on would not be enclosed by two doors, but instead would have a fall-flap that exactly covered that arrangement of drawers in the top half, a fall-flap with folding iron support which hinged back into the inside of the cabinet. This flap falls right down and forms a tremendously large writing surface. Again this is quite a desirable piece of furniture.

Now I want to redefine the descriptions of these rather similar pieces for you. A bureau-bookcase always has a sloping front to the bureau – with a nest of drawers and pigeon-holes inside. It's definitely a bookcase upon a bureau. A secretaire-bookcase always has a pull-out drawer which has a front that falls down and the same fittings within. Then, as we've seen, just as you get a bureau without a bookcase top, so you can have a secretaire-chest without the bookcase top. This meets exactly the same purpose and you could say a secretaire-chest is the exact equivalent of a bureau.

Now, an escritoire – and you get them in walnut or occasionally later in mahogany – always has a great fall-flap. If instead of the flap there's a pair of doors it becomes a cabinet. *90* is round about 1710-20 and is veneered in walnut. Practically all of them conform to this outline although an earlier one might be veneered in oyster-shell and inlaid with those well-known geometrical designs in holly.

This arrangement of a central cupboard door and a surround of small drawers is always found to be much the same on cabinets or escritoires made from say 1690 to about 1730 or 1740 at the latest. There are usually some secret drawers. If we talk of the *90* type, usually behind those two top drawers there are one or two very tiny little drawers. With another arrangement of the interior of cabinets and escritoires, those two top drawers are not there, but instead a row of, as it were, boxed pigeon-holes. When I say boxed pigeon-holes I mean little upright pigeon-holes which can be removed in sections of three, more or less as drawers. And again behind them there would be secret drawers. Of course these interiors change in the manner of production but never really in their arrangement. For example, sometimes on a superb piece of furniture you may find the central door having carved Corinthian columns to either side. These again would contain secret drawers. They could be pulled out.

90 Queen Anne cabinet, *c*.1715

They're always retained in these early pieces by hidden springs. Some-times it's very difficult to find the little spring that will release the secret. This is a type of secret drawer which is no longer secret. You find them in these little columns inside bureaux. They're nearly always pull-out drawers, always hiding secret recesses, but by now everybody knows about them.

80 has them behind its sloping front. I've opened many, many secret
drawers, that perhaps have not been opened for ages, and I've never found
anything of any consequence in any of them. But I have often found £5 and
£10 and £1 notes in the fly-leaves of books in libraries. This seemed to be a
popular place for an owner to slip a few notes if they wished to secrete
them somewhere.

Following in the line of bookcases, secretaires, escritoires and so on, there
are larger bookcases, such as shown in *91*, library bookcases. They usually
have a break-front. This description 'break-front' often puzzles people. It
doesn't mean that the front is broken in the sense that it's damaged. It just
means that there is a break in the straight line and that can be seen by close
examination of the moulding on the cornice. You see the centre part does
just protrude a couple of inches from the straight line and, although this
bookcase itself doesn't show it, such bookcases often have a secretaire
drawer in the centre of the middle portion. It's a deep drawer just as I've
described in secretaires, with the front of the drawer falling down and
little fittings of pigeon-holes and drawers behind. And of course this makes
them much more useful and much more desirable, because it serves a dual
purpose in a library. This bookcase, in mahogany, is of superb quality. The
veneer on the drawer fronts is really remarkable and another feature of a
bookcase such as this lies in the oval astragals to the glazed doors.

You know it is a curious thing how so many people are under the im-
pression that a glazed astragal door has to have thirteen panes of glass.
Many times I have been stopped and told, 'I have a bookcase, it's very,
very rare because it has Chippendale's thirteen-pane glass door.' I suppose
Chippendale's thirteen-pane glass door, this arrangement of astragals which
is so well known and which in fact has thirteen panes of glass, is about the
most common. When you come to a bookcase such as this (possibly Hepplewhite) you see this man has gone to a lot more trouble, not just framing
square pieces of astragal to form the well-known design of the thirteen-
pane door, but actually bending these astragals into ovals.

There are many different astragals on doors, which add a terrific sum of
money to the article on which they appear, simply because they are *not*
thirteen-pane glazed doors, but are in fact doors with very pretty shaped
bars, often inlaid, sometimes inlaid with cable, black and white cable lines,
sometimes even having carved flower-heads at the little intersections, so

very much more work than the thirteen-pane door on which everyone seems to set such store.

It is fascinating to watch a cabinet-maker make these doors. To start with you have just the rectangular inch-wide outline of the door and nothing but space in the middle. This frame is usually pinned down on a board on a bench, and then the pieces of what is known as astragal moulding are fitted – in this case these lovely ovals which have to be patiently built up. These would probably be made in half segments and then pinned face downwards on the board, just lightly glued together and left in that way. Behind each of these shapes there is a little groove into which had then to be fitted a three-eighth or a half-inch deep piece of wood to brace the astragals, and bear in mind all had to be cut to shape and fitted beautifully.

When this was fixed and dry it formed the rabbet for the thin Eighteenth-century panes of glass. These also had to be cut and fixed into the rabbets with putty which kept the glass firm, and when that had been done these doors were extremely strong. It is remarkable to see a door frame with nothing inside it, just a bare outline of about one-inch wood being built up with tiny thin pieces of wood, and then the fillet going in the back of the thing to form the rabbet, and then the glass and then the putty. Then it was all taken off the bench and you have a most rigid door.

This glass was lovely, thin, twelve-ounce glass. I love to see old glass in these bookcases, because it's by no means flat. It tends to bend and it's certainly got a grain. If you look across the glass front of an old bookcase, not only is it slightly bowed but it's definitely got a grain and is so desirable that it's a great shame when old pieces of glass of this nature are actually thrown away. What these old-time cabinet-makers used in the way of putty I've no idea. But if you've tried, as I have often, to remove that old putty in order to let in a new piece of glass you realise that you've got something very akin to concrete to deal with.

You'll notice here a rather common feature in a cornice, a sort of a Gothic, tiny church window effect up the top there, those little finials, pear-drops we call them. That's called a Gothic pear-drop cornice. You'll notice the cupboards in the centre of the base. Here you have again a solid panel door with a moulded astragal. The usual broken corners have been filled in rather prettily with anthemion or honeysuckle. It gives a very pleasant effect and the whole adds up to an extremely attractive library bookcase.

92 shows yet another bookcase, a simple low-standing bookcase. Today we're very accustomed to seeing bookcases with open shelves, that is with no doors at all or with sliding glass doors, but here is a nice type of Regency bookcase about 1810 to 1820 in rosewood, very simple, and yet rather attractive. Not just squares between the glazed doors, but little fluted columns with moulded capitals, just to elevate it a little from the simple sort of thing; not plain ends you see, but sunk panelled ends, and those rather pretty turned feet.

This is a type of bookcase which is rather nice. And of course invariably they have the loose scagliola marble top. These loose marble tops originated, I suppose, with William Kent. Those massive side-tables or enormous hall tables, those big commodes, they all invariably carried thick Italian marble tops – some of them extremely fine. And it went on right through the Eighteenth century, particularly with the French furniture of

92 Regency break-front bookcase, c.1815

Louis XVI, most of their standing furniture having marble tops. But of late marble has fallen from grace in homes. People do not like this cold surface. But it is a curious thing how, if the marble top has been replaced with wood, in exactly the same form and thickness, for some reason or the other the piece of furniture does lose a lot of its character. And perhaps people who might not have much knowledge of furniture would say, 'Doesn't that look funny? Maybe this is all that has happened to it – that the marble has been taken away, an exactly similar wooden top of the same thickness has been substituted, and yet it doesn't look the part.

Mirrors

Turning to mirrors I find these very interesting because they occupied an important place in homes, much the same as chairs did. You find glass coming into the country or being made in London, at Vauxhall in the middle of the Seventeenth century, and so it's possible to find mirrors which take up all the style points of the contemporary pieces of furniture. What I mean by that is this. You can find a Charles II mirror, usually rectangular, in a walnut frame, the frame pierced and carved, so that if you took any one of its four sides you could almost use it as the top-rail of a Charles II chair. It will have the same idea running right through it. Always little cherubs, and a crown or something heraldic in the centre. The crown always had these little cherub supporters in Charles's time.

A bit earlier you get mirrors with needlework borders, because there was a profusion of needlework done by people in the Seventeenth century. You find them making rectangular frames, and enclosing in the centre panel a piece of mirror, with a needlework border. Right through the Eighteenth century the same style of mirror was made. You know the type which has a solid top and bottom with shaped ear-pieces, usually the top carved with a gilt shell or a gilt bird. These were made right through the

93 George I mirror, *c.* 1720

Eighteenth century. You get them in the early stages, in the first twenty or thirty years, in walnut, always the mouldings cross-grained, but with just the same outlines as the later ones in mahogany. You get the closed shell on the walnut ones, and on George I and George II mirrors. Then you get the closed shell taken away and a bird carved in the surmount, and gilt, and this type of mirror was really, I suppose, very popular, because there seem to be many of them about.

93 shows a really attractive George I mirror. This style of outer frame line is well known. You see it has a narrow gilt border to the cross-grained walnut frame which is this mysterious thing called gesso. It just means that the pine moulding has been carved and then given an application by brushwork of a thin film of plaster of Paris. Then, when the right amount of body is on the raw wood, a gilder would come along and sharpen up some of the edges and then, with some mordant like linseed oil, would put the 22-carat gold leaf on. You see down the sides of this mirror there's a little appliqué carving of oak-leaves and acorns in wood and, of course, it carries this early type of swan-neck cornice with the large central cartouche.

The whole of the woodwork of mirrors such as 93 is nearly always in pine and then everything else is laid on top of it. Pine was deliberately chosen: not only for easier gilding but also for easier veneering. This is veneered in walnut, cross-grained most of the way round and, because the pine was soft, so much the better was the veneer able to adhere to it.

Many of these mirrors have, of course, come to need new mirror plates and, if there is a bevelled plate in the mirror, it is a pretty safe thing to say that if you run your forefinger down the bevelling, you should not be able to feel it. This is a tip by which you can know it is an old mirror plate. In this particular wall mirror the plate is not bevelled, so you hold the point of a pencil to the actual mirror until it touches. In this case the image of the pencil seems to be about one-eighth of an inch from the point of the pencil itself. That means that this is a thin mirror plate and is probably old – especially if it gives a dark reflection.

If one sees the image of the point of a pencil in a mirror a quarter of an inch or more away from the actual point, this means that it's the thick, much later, quarter-plate glass with a painted back. All the early mirrors had what is known as raw silver backs. They were not painted as they are today. You can handle a modern mirror more easily, but with these old

mirrors, if you handle them, you have to be careful not to touch any part
of the raw silver back with your fingers because off comes the silver; it
adheres in a moment to the finger-tips and then you have just nasty round
blotches of naked glass. This then becomes known as a distressed mirror.

Here is another upright wall mirror (94). Here you have what is known
as shaped ear-pieces. This is in walnut. You'll notice the cross-graining
of the moulded frame. A little bit of carved gesso edging to the mirror and
then, up above, a carved open shell with those applied pieces. Now all that
is veneered on pine. These mirrors are always in deal. Rather pretty picked

curls again, the graining matching on both sides of the shell. You can see on the one hand the veneer laid this way and then reversed and turned over, to get that figuring to correspond each side. This mirror, of course, is approximately the same date as 93 but quite obviously it didn't cost anything like the amount of money. One can see the difference in these two mirrors, the carved drapery down the side of 93 and the whole set-up with that bold swan-neck cornice and big applied mouldings all carved with gesso, as against this rather simple, but very attractive mirror (94). These were made right on through the Eighteenth century, probably up to 1780 in mahogany, just to the same outline. Some have a closed shell at the top, though most of the mahogany ones don't. They usually have a carved gilt bird.

Of course Chippendale really went to town on some of the frames of mirrors during the last half of the Eighteenth century, and so did Robert Adam. Robert Adam introduced his familiar motifs onto mirror frames too. These lovely swags of drapery and ribbons, oval patera, bluebell drops, all in carved wood, very shapey, neo-classic designs, but I think some of the finest mirrors are to be found in the designs of Thomas Chippendale. He nearly always utilised rectangular-shaped plates. Sometimes these had outer mirror borders, but invariably the one frame was carved with all sorts of C scrolls, foliage and oft-times with a carved cartouche on the top, as a sort of surmount.

It's remarkable too that, for all the rectangular-shaped mirrors, there are only a few that have oval plates. Now look at 95, this oval gilt Chippendale mirror. There it is, all carved in pine. All those C scrolls, those acanthus leaves growing up, as it were, outside the oval frames, but he was clever enough to drop an odd one or two across the moulded frame, tying it, tying the acanthus to the actual mirror frame. And you notice the C scrolls. This man was very fond of introducing the C scrolls everywhere he could. You get them under the brackets on Chippendale chair legs, and you certainly get them all round his mirror frames.

You see the big carved Cs on the top of this mirror, with that crowning piece of acanthus rising up, and you notice an unusual feature at the base, a little dolphin, just sitting in there, tied onto the mirror by his tail. This is what Chippendale liked to do. There was a man named Johnson,[1] who

[1] Thomas Johnson, carver, c. 1755, of Grafton St, Soho.

95 Chippendale carved gilt mirror, *c.*1770

96 Chippendale carved gilt mirror, *c*.1760

used to specialise in mirrors, and there's an extremely fine pair of mirrors in Corsham Court where the actual foliage passes through the mirror frame, intertwined as though it had grown around it. It goes in and out, in and out all the way up those rather large oval mirrors. They're superb mirrors, as is this one. You get all sorts of different little motifs introduced on mirror frames, but basically acanthus, with fruit and flowers and all the bold C scrolls.

You see in 96 a typical Chippendale mirror. Once again it has outer mirror borders all the way round it, top, bottom and sides, but all with the same carved C scroll motifs, with the acanthus once more, used in a sort of strap-work manner, so that it links not only the outer mirrors, but ties it back to the rectangular mirror in the centre of it all. Nothing unusual at the bottom, but rather a nice basket of flowers, and foliage in the very top of the mirror. That's a good example of a mirror with these outer mirror borders.

Now 97 shows a profusely carved Chippendale mirror, obviously Chippendale, again with two plates, this time one above the other. This is known as a two-plate upright mirror. You see the sort of perpendicular architecture type of support, with the dripping water, as it's called, frozen water carving dripping down off C scrolls. Just a little hint of pierced fret above and below the dripping water, and again absolutely smothered with C scrolls everywhere, English rococo at its best. The foliage at the sides is growing right up, and you've even got tree-trunks here, with branches and leaves shooting out from the main stems. And these two exotic birds, caught as though they had just alighted on the picture frames. In fact they almost seem alive. They're sitting there as though they are just about to peck at the leaves of the carved acanthus. Then way up more scrolls, profusely carved again, and a sort of finial, very like the finial on the oval mirror which we first talked about (95). Of course these upright mirrors are rather large. This one is about seven foot overall from the top to the bottom, and is an extremely important mirror.

All these mirrors have gilt frames, and one is asked so often what one can do with the gold when it's actually worn. Well, in my view the best thing to do is to leave them severely alone, because one seems to forget that these gilt mirrors were actually gilt in 22-carat gold leaf. No bronze paint; really gold leaf, put on in much the same way as was the gesso on early gesso tables. That's to say the pine has to have a preparation of something upon it, so that the gold leaf will more readily adhere. It won't stick on plain wood, and so a preparation has to be made of some sort of plaster of Paris with precipitated chalk. You brush the raw wood frame with this plaster solution, and you allow that to dry. Then when it's dry you do the same operation once again and again and again (and you do it by simple brush-work) until you've got sufficient on for your purpose. A gesso table has to be built up much more than an ordinary mirror frame, because the gesso on a table usually has to be carved, so sufficient plaster has to be put on to allow the edges to be cut clean again. If this is properly done, when the gold is actually put on you have the fine design of the sharp edges, but these mirrors would only carry a coating of plaster of Paris and then some amalgam or linseed oil is put on so that the gold leaf adheres to it.

Then the gold leaf is picked up with a very fine brush. A man who is used to gilding would do that this way. He would rub the brush once or twice across his cheek, and with the little bit of moisture that the hairs would pick up, he would transfer one of these flimsy gold leaves and attach it to wherever he would like to lay it upon the mirror, and so he would eventually cover up the whole of the wood with gold leaf. The surplus gold would be brushed off, and there you would have a mirror – when it was new – in a fine outer gold frame.

All these outer mirror frames were in pine or some soft wood, obviously to help the carver. It would be almost impossible to carve one of these pierced mirror frames in, say, wainscot oak. Not only that but pine is also much more absorbent than shiny wainscot oak – and this makes the process of gilding easier. You see the mirror in 98 obviously has an earlier type of frame. William Kent, this. Again in gold, all in soft wood. You get his Italian influence there, with a female mask on the frieze and this architectural cornice boldly carved as with all his things, with that egg and tongue moulding and the big central cartouche. It's all beautifully gilt, all adds up to a mirror of about 1730. And you can see, by comparing these two mirrors, the transition from William Kent (involved with the rather heavy baroque period), his frame being all solid wood apart from a little cable running down the side – the transition through Chippendale, whose mirrors were pierced and carved (and still a bit costly and very lively and

rather ornate) down even still further to Hepplewhite, whose mirrors had practically no frame at all.

The round mirror, the convex mirror, these came much later. I don't suppose there are very many before about 1800. They usually all take the same form, a wide, round frame, enclosing a convex mirror. And for some reason or other there's nearly always an eagle – a carved eagle – as a surmount over these mirrors. 99 shows the eagle with a glass ball suspended

98 William Kent
carved gilt mirror, c.1730

from its mouth. Again we see the pieces of carved acanthus at the side, the ball-enriched frame which is quite usual, and rather a nice little pair of candle brackets to either side. The convex mirror, of course, would reflect the light from the candles and help to illuminate the room.

Now that's not a bad type of mirror, and you may wonder why such a mirror is always hung in dining-rooms. Now there is a reason for this. You see, a butler can stand a little to the side of the mirror and watch reflected in it the whole of the dining-room. He can see everyone's plate, he can see everyone's wine-glass without going round and bothering them; and he can then give his instructions to the footmen and maids, that down there

100 Georgian convex mirror, *c.*1805

a glass needs refilling or over here there's something else needs doing. And this is why they're always hung over a fireplace, or a wall over the sideboard, close to where a butler might take up a position with this end in view.

Now these mirrors, as I've said, are always very, very similar and usually there's not all that much to choose from among them. They don't always have the candle branches, but they are certainly always round. They nearly always have a ball-enriched frame, although this is not one hundred per cent true. But they're all of that form. And yet every now and then along comes a mirror which is apt to put every other one more or less in the shade, such as *100*. Now if you compare these two convex mirrors, you can't help finding *100* so much the more lively that it's almost impossible. That nine- or ten-inch-wide frame is so profusely pierced and carved with flower-heads, fruit and foliage, and everything else, and then there is the build-up of that rocky device there, again with the carved eagle sitting on top. This comparison shows what an extremely rare convex mirror looks like.

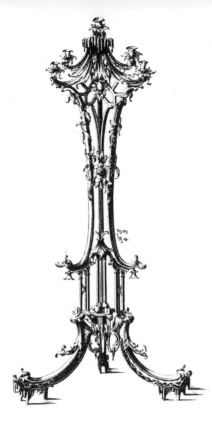

Odds and ends

Now I would like to show you some interesting items. Of course, pieces of furniture got put to different purposes by design. The great man who played about, as it were, with known examples of furniture was Thomas Sheraton. Here was a man who made composite pieces of furniture, pieces that could serve one, two, or even three purposes. I've seen Pembroke tables which outwardly were ordinary two-flap mahogany tables. Pull the drawer out and touch a spring and up at one end shoots a fitted compartment for stationery, inks, writing materials and the lot, and virtually turns an ordinary Pembroke table into a writing-table. Again you have the little so-called *bonheur-de-jour*-a piece at which a lady can sort of pop down at any time of the day and write a little note; again with a folding top which opens out, green baize-lined, again for writing.

Sheraton's adaptation of tables and chairs into library steps is very well known. In *101* you can envisage this set of steps closed down. Here then you would see a rectangular shaped mahogany table with, on the long sides, a knee-hole which obviously could be used as a writing-table. Just by touching a spring the top is released and, as it were, stands upright to reveal folding steps inside. And not only that, the supports which hold the top up in fact become the handrails to the library steps. I feel sure that everyone will agree this is most ingenious and this, I suppose, is what Thomas Sheraton will be remembered for.

101 Sheraton library steps, *c.*1795

102 Chippendale 3-tier dumb waiter, *c.*1770

102 shows a dumb waiter. These, I suppose, came to their perfection in the time of Chippendale. This is a particularly good example. You see the long column supporting the trays – it's spirally carved in vase shape. This is often the type of stem used on tripod tables and it's a very pretty effect. And there it goes, right down to the tripod feet. You'll notice now that these are really remarkable. Normally tripods on dumb waiters are quite plain, for they were working pieces of furniture without doubt, but this one is a little bit better than most in that it's carved with acanthus right down over the knee and half-way down the leg with a very good example of a claw gripping a ball properly. You can see just a trace of the C scrolls under the tops of the legs, where they join the column. Normally these things have three revolving trays like this one, sometimes only two. Sometimes they are hinged, and have two little flaps which fall down, and very occasionally, like this example, the trays have little galleries made of turned spindles, with a nice moulded top-rail. And all that adds up to an extremely unusual and rare piece of furniture. I think it's true to say that

197

103 Late Sheraton oval wine-cooler and jardinière, c.1805

these trays always revolve, at least all the genuine ones I've seen do so.

103 shows rather an interesting wine-cooler, and a matching open wine-cooler or jardinière. You see they're obviously made by the same hand—these are just about on the turn of the century, perhaps 1805, since they're inlaid with a black line (supposedly in mourning for Nelson). And it's rather unusual I think to get what might be called a matching pair of things like this. Here you have the closed wine-cooler, lead-lined, probably with a little tap underneath to get rid of all the surplus water when the ice had melted, carrying handles on the sides and mounted on those rather sturdy tapered legs, with the brass cup castors for added strengthening. Sturdy legs are very necessary, because quite obviously, when this gets filled with about fourteen bottles packed with ice, it's carrying a lot of weight. But to my mind that's a nice chubby piece of furniture, looks nice and inviting. And it is very unusual to have a matching jardinière en suite with it. These things are sometimes called open wine-coolers—they are in fact made just like wine-coolers, some of them also lead-lined, but they have no lid and never did have. But this is possibly a jardinière because you notice it has no carrying handles, and the legs are perhaps just a trifle less sturdy. And curiously enough, although it's obviously en suite, the castors have been changed – they're not cup castors, but just little ordinary brass wheel castors.

You see in *104* two rather peculiar pieces of furniture – both Jacobean. Even if you didn't know what they were for, by intuition and deduction you might get round to it, for these are in fact little things into which you can pop a child to help it and to teach it to walk. The one I like particularly – these are two quite distinct pieces of furniture – the one I like is the round one – on those heavy wooden castors. I can see that child standing up in there and toddling about by pushing this baby-cage (that's its official name) about the room, and so gaining confidence to walk on its own two legs.

Now, the long rectangular-shaped one is not portable. It has the frame-work of a long joint stool, and although I do not know this piece of furniture, I feel absolutely convinced that that square piece of wood with the hole in the middle slides in a groove from one end to the other, thereby in this manner teaching the child to gain confidence and to toddle from end to end. But for my money I like the round one because the little mite can push

104 Two baby carriages, *c.*1680 and 1700

this all round the room, rather than being self-contained in that rather rectangular-shaped cage. Of course the rectangular one perhaps has a practical advantage because it stops the child from getting into mischief by working its way over to another piece of furniture which perhaps has a precious vase standing on it. All the same I prefer the round one.

Of course cabinet-makers had young boys articled to them as apprentices learning the trade, and to my mind these apprentices are responsible for some rare, miniature pieces of furniture, usually referred to as samples, but erroneously so I think. I'm of the opinion that these miniature pieces of furniture such as *105* are the work of an apprentice passing out as it were, making something to show that he was now fully qualified as a cabinet-maker.

105 Miniature tallboy

106 Miniature bureau-bookcase

Now that little miniature tallboy is in mahogany and is a queer little thing. It's only about 12 inches wide, but you see how it's got things which already tie back to other pieces of furniture which have been mentioned in this book. You notice on the very bottom drawers, in the centre of both the top and the bottom parts, there is again reproduced a very pretty sunburst, and right at the very top, here again, you have a swan-neck cornice with those two large flower-heads, exactly the same as we saw in the rather fine bureau-bookcase (80) and also in very similar fashion on the early George I mirror (93).

106 shows us another apprentice piece. Here is a fellow passing out of his apprenticeship in, say, 1710–15, used to working in walnut, making a miniature bureau-bookcase more or less to his own design. You notice it has a queer sort of square-cut corner in the top of the mirror but, nevertheless, it's good quality. He's showing off, as it were, inlaying a bit too profusely, but showing off his qualifications and ability to become a recognised cabinet-maker.

201

Appendices

Pointers

The dating of antiques is half the fun of appreciating them. Some are easy: some present considerable problems (e.g. *80*, p. 163). Apart from the firm classical signposts about which there is no doubt, by listening to and sifting expert opinion, and by personal observation, one gradually develops over the years one's own recognition system. It is impossible to give hard and fast rules, since there are always exceptions, but one of the best ways of identifying a table or chair is by its legs. So you will find, on pp. 210–12, drawings which clearly show the better known styles from the bulbous legs of the Elizabethan refectory table up to the sabre-shaped leg of 1815, and you wouldn't go far wrong if you used this section alone.

But there are, of course, other ways of recognising and dating a piece of furniture, most of which I have mentioned in this book. For quick reference let me repeat them here.

Pointers to period

General

Different woods were used at different times. Mahogany for instance does not appear before about 1730. 18th-century mahogany is much heavier and naturally much darker than 19th-century mahogany. A chart showing the woods which were being used at any one time can be found on p. 214.

Staining is a sign of lateness. The unpolished undersides of period pieces should show raw wood, only slightly darkened by age.

White edges show on reproductions. Repeated cleaning removes the stain on corners.

The Tudor rose appears frequently on 16th- and 17th-century pieces (*6*).

Pierced carving of a crown with cherub supporters is a Carolean motif (*6*).

Early mouldings from 1690 to the introduction of mahogany are worked cross-grain (*94*).

18th-century pieces, particularly chairs and bookcases, sometimes had Roman numerals cut into the centre of the backs of seat-rails or into shelves for identification.

Cluster-column legs are a sign of Chippendale (*59*). Open cluster-column legs (*52*) are a few years earlier than the solid cluster.

Hair-claw feet are George II (*14*).

Vase-turned stems (*56*) date from *c.* 1760 to *c.* 1860, getting progressively heavier in design as time passes.

Veneers. Where the veneer is broken, close study will show that the earlier the piece, the thicker the veneer.

Period pieces that have been properly cared for acquire a surface character or 'patina' that can be recognised. Outlines tend to have a period form. Like patina this can be recognised.

Chairs

Springing in seats was first introduced in the Nineteenth century.

Chairs and stools of the same period are always matching.

Chair-leg designs of the Seventeenth century, whether spiral or turned, are usually repeated in the uprights (*6*).

The cherub motif usually found on the top-rails is often repeated on mirror frames and clock spandrels of this period.

Straight-leg chairs which have no stretchers are usually Hepplewhite (*29*).

Straight-leg chairs always had stretchers before *c.* 1770.

Tables

An extending dining-table worked by a screw cannot be earlier than William IV (1830–37).

Multiple-pillar dining-tables (*48*) are invariably made in mahogany.

Early sofa-tables on end-standards (*63*) or tables that stand on central columns with tripod or quadruple supports (*56*) should have legs coming straight off the columns. When they have 'bumps' where the legs join the columns (*48*) they are later. The larger or more pronounced the bumps the later they are – the whole range dating from 1780–1850.

Sideboards
A sideboard has six legs, a dressing-table four – otherwise they may appear very similar.
Sheraton was the first designer to make a sideboard in one piece.

Drawers and drawer-construction
(a) If made before *c.*1730 the grain of the bottom board runs lengthwise.
(b) If made after *c.*1730 the grain of the bottom board runs crosswise.
(c) If there is a quadrant beading running along the joints of side and bottom boards the drawer certainly belongs to a 19th-century piece.

The thicker and coarser the sides of a drawer and the dovetails are, the earlier it is. The thinner and finer they are, the later in the Eighteenth century they are – the finest of all being almost invariably Hepplewhite and Sheraton.

Drawers that are nailed together, rather than dovetailed or glued, usually are found on Dutch pieces.

Cock Beads
Small projecting mouldings applied around all four edges of drawer-fronts. This method was not introduced till about 1730, before which the under-mentioned applied:
Before about 1650 Drawers were made by dovetailing the sides of the drawer fronts so that these dovetails showed right through the front of each drawer.
Circa 1650 The same method applied but the dovetails no longer showed through the drawer-front.
Circa 1660 Drawers were made in the same manner but now the drawer-fronts had mitred mouldings applied all over them in various geometrical designs.
Circa 1690 The drawers were still dovetailed as hitherto but now the carcase edges that frame the drawers (called partition edges) have a small bead moulding worked on them – the drawer fronts remaining quite flat.
Circa 1710 The drawers constructed as before but the drawer-fronts now protruded over the partition edges. The protrusions had a narrow moulding worked on them and when the drawers were shut, this moulding overlapped these partition edges.

Circa 1730 Cock beads (described above) were introduced and continued throughout the Eighteenth century.

Mirrors
(a) In the first 30 years of the Eighteenth century mirror frames were almost invariably in walnut and at that period there was usually a gilt shell in the central cartouche.
(b) If the mirror plates are old, you can scarcely feel the bevelling on the edge.
(c) If an old mirror plate is touched with a pencil the point will almost touch its reflection. The later the plate, the wider the gap.

Castors
*c.*1700–hard wooden wheels in wooden axles.
*c.*1750–first use of leather rollers.
*c.*1770–introduction of brass cylinder castors in many stock styles and sizes.

Handles
The various styles of handle are shown on p. 213. Of course, the handles, like castors, may very well not be the original ones, and indeed were often changed if fashion dictated (e.g. the Victorian wooden knob). Early handles were held on by a split pin. The use of nut and bolt does not come in until the Eighteenth century.

Designers
Cluster-column legs are Chippendale (*52*).

Hepplewhite chairs usually have no stretchers (*29*).

Hepplewhite used Prince of Wales plumes as a motif in his designs (*26*).

Hepplewhite used heart-shaped backs to his chairs (*25*).

The ribbon tie is really an Adam motif but is oft-times incorporated by Hepplewhite (*26*).

Sheraton chairs usually have stretchers (*31*).

Thomas Sheraton used inlays extensively (*61*).

Pointers to pretence

Ball-and-claw feet should be strongly carved showing plenty of wood and with the ball firmly grasped (56). If it is not but looks weak and skimpy it probably means that it has been re-carved at a later date out of a pad foot.

If a joint can be seen between the edge of a pie-crust table and the main board it means the pie-crust has been added later. An original pie-crust would have been carved out of the same solid piece.

The diameter of a tripod table top should roughly equal the spread of its feet (58). If not, it may be a marriage of convenience.

If one or two parts of a piece are a different colour to the rest then they are almost certainly repairs.

If two halves (or top and bottom) of a piece (e.g. a secretaire-bookcase) have decoration motifs that do not exactly match or the colour of the wood is different, it is another marriage of convenience.

Front seat-rails in armchairs belonging to a set should be 2–3″ wider than the seat-rails of the single chairs.

Three-section dining-tables on 12 to 16 legs (47) have often been split up. The parts can be recognised, if found separately, by the give-away slots in the edges (pp. 105–6).

Pointers to value

General
Good style and line.
Quality and extra decorative work (use of veneers).
Rarity.
Usefulness.

Armchairs
Arms that are shaped and show wood rather than being stuffed.
Sets of chairs that have been 'armed' up have less value.

Tables
Rule joints usually show extra quality.

Chests
If the overall quality is the same then values will vary in the following order: serpentine (the most expensive). concave, bow-front and straight-front.

Carving
Deep and crisp with freedom of design.

Legs

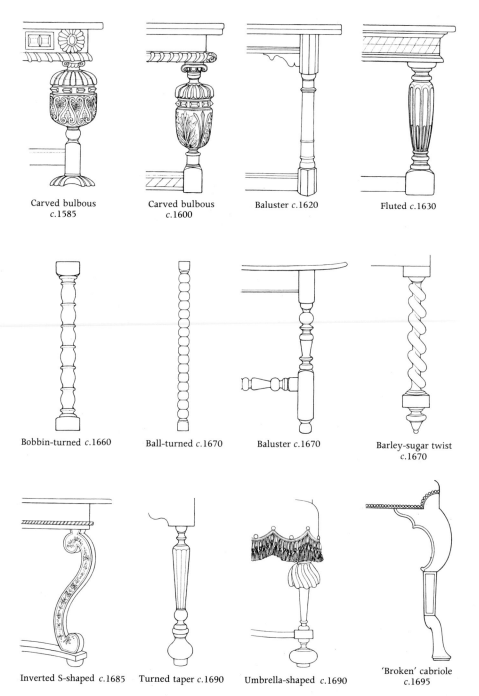

Carved bulbous
c.1585

Carved bulbous
c.1600

Baluster c.1620

Fluted c.1630

Bobbin-turned c.1660

Ball-turned c.1670

Baluster c.1670

Barley-sugar twist
c.1670

Inverted S-shaped c.1685

Turned taper c.1690

Umbrella-shaped c.1690

'Broken' cabriole
c.1695

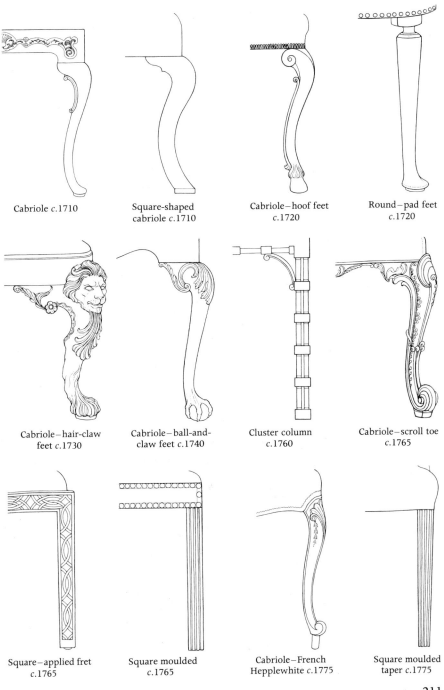

Cabriole c.1710

Square-shaped
cabriole c.1710

Cabriole – hoof feet
c.1720

Round – pad feet
c.1720

Cabriole – hair-claw
feet c.1730

Cabriole – ball-and-
claw feet c.1740

Cluster column
c.1760

Cabriole – scroll toe
c.1765

Square – applied fret
c.1765

Square moulded
c.1765

Cabriole – French
Hepplewhite c.1775

Square moulded
taper c.1775

211

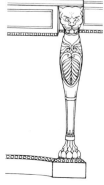

Square taper–spade
feet c.1775

'Hepplewhite' turned
c.1780

Sphinx c.1805

Monopodium c.1810

Feet on chests

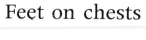

Sabre or Trafalgar-
shaped c.1815

Late 17th century: ball

stump

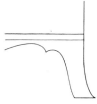

18th century: bracket

splay

ogee

212

Handles

(a) Cast

Axe-drop *c.*1700

Pear-drop *c.*1700

Acorn-drop *c.*1700

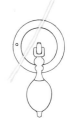

Drop-handle *c.*1700

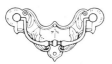

Solid engraved plate
*c.*1710

Solid shaped plate
*c.*1710

Pierced plate *c.*1720

Pierced plate *c.*1765

Swan-neck 1760-1800

**(b) Stamped from
sheet brass 1790-1820**

Round ring

Oval plate

Swan-neck with stamped roses

Lion-mask ring

213

Time Chart

PERIOD	APPROX DATES	WOODS USED	FRENCH PERIODS
Elizabethan	1550–1603	Solid heavy oak and plain solid walnut	Henri IV
Stuart	1603–49 (James I Charles I)	Solid oak and solid walnut	Louis XIII
Cromwellian	1649–1660 Commonwealth and the Protectorate	Oak – upholstery leather	Louis XIV
Carolean	1660–1689 (Charles II & James II)	Walnut, beech, carved oak. Cane introduced to chairs. Marquetry developing	Louis XIV
William & Mary	1689–1702 William & Mary & William III	Veneers – burr walnut, laburnum and yew. Gesso introduced and lacquer, geometrical designs in inlay	Louis XIV
Queen Anne	1702–14	Veneers – burr walnut, mulberry, yew – cabriole legs extensively used – oak	Louis XIV
Early Georgian	1714–1745	The 'Baroque' period. William Kent – walnut veneers, gesso, red walnut. Mahogany from 1730	French Regency 1715–23 Louis XV
Chippendale	1745–1779	The 'Rococo' period. Finest Spanish mahogany – fine carving – Chinese influence	Louis XV
Adam	1762–1792	The 'Neo-classic' period. Fine inlays of tulipwood, satinwood, amboyna etc, in mahogany. Satinwood introduced and in favour. Painted furniture	Louis XV & Louis XVI
Hepplewhite (died 1786)	1770–1794	'Graceful' furniture – mahogany principally. Use of japanning re-introduced. French influence	Louis XV & Louis XVI
Sheraton	1790–1806	Mahogany, satinwood and rosewood. Plentiful use of inlay	Louis XVI
Regency	1806–1820	Mahogany and rosewood, brass inlay. Egyptian motifs introduced	Empire
Late Georgian	1820–1837	Regency styles becoming much heavier in form – papier-mâché furniture	Louis XVIII
Victorian	1837–1870	Victorian 'Gothic' introduced. Very heavy designs – much wood used.	

Glossary

ACANTHUS Carving of a conventional leaf decoration.

ANTHEMION An ornament of decoration resembling a honeysuckle flower – oft-times appears as an inlay.

ART NOUVEAU This name refers to a late Victorian style, at its best from 1895 to 1905, of designs coming from Europe as well as England. Messrs Tiffany's of New York & Messrs Liberty's of London did much to encourage this movement and held large stocks of the articles which were made in glass, pottery, pewter, silver, and other materials.

ASTRAGAL A narrow moulding used for glazing-bars in bookcases.

BALL-AND-CLAW Wood carved to represent a claw clutching a ball.

BALL-TURNED A kind of turned baluster formed of round balls, as it were, one on top of the other.

BALUSTER The shape of a turned leg or a turned pillar of a tripod table–something like the stem of a wine glass.

BARLEY-SUGAR TWIST Another form of baluster leg in the form of a spiral.

BAROQUE The style given to furniture made during the late 17th and early 18th Centuries – usually very heavy in detail, with extravagant curves and large mask-heads.

BAT'S-WING FLUTING Gadroons that are graduated and curved and do resemble a bat's wing.

BEARER The two small squares of wood that pull out to support bureau flaps or similar hinged flaps on top of chests, etc.

BENCH-BOOK A book giving cabinet-makers directions on how to construct furniture.

BIRD-CAGE FITTING An extra strong under-carriage for a tip-up table, formed by 2 squares of wood held together by 4 small turned columns, the whole being on a pedestal leg.

BLIND FRET Fretwork that is not pierced through (either carved or applied).

BOBBIN-TURN A form of baluster turned to represent a bobbin (like a ball-turned baluster) one bobbin on top of the other.

BRACKETS Generally used to 'tie' a leg to the supporting rail either on chairs or tables.

BRACKET FOOT A type of foot upon which a piece of furniture stands – usually straight – when moulded called an ogee foot.

BREAK-FRONT The protruding centre portion of a bookcase that has side sections.

CABRIOLE A curved leg of elongated S form curved outward at the top, gradually tapering to a round or pointed toe–usually round but sometimes square.

CANTED CORNERS Bevelled corners – sometimes reeded, sometimes fluted, sometimes left quite plain.

CARTOUCHE A decorative device, perhaps being an Escutcheon of Arms, usually in the centres of cornices or large tables.

CARYATID A carved female figure used as an ornament or decoration or even as a leg of this form.

215

CHAMFER The bevelled edge (usually on a chair leg) cut off from a square. Perhaps a plan will show it best – it is on the inside of the leg to make it look a little less heavy:

CLUSTER COLUMN Usually three turned spindles clustered together as decoration or to form legs of tables or chairs.

CRESTING-RAIL See top-rail.

CROSS-GRAIN MOULDING The moulding is worked across the grain of the wood.

DENTIL Moulding on a cornice looking like a row of teeth.

DISTRESSED Relates to any piece of furniture in very poor condition – and particularly to the glass in mirrors.

DOVETAILED The method used by a cabinet-maker to join drawer-sides – something like teeth that interlock between the drawer's front and the sides.

END-STANDARDS Solid or pierced ends to a table or stool – used in differing forms from the 16th to the 19th Century.

ESCRITOIRE A cabinet with fitted drawers enclosed by a fall-front flap used for writing.

FAMILLE ROSE The name of the very popular pink enamel decoration extensively used by the Chinese on their export porcelain in the 18th Century, from about 1720 when this European enamel was first introduced to China. Hence *famille rose* porcelain.

FINIAL A small turned ornament to be found at the intersection of some stretchers under chairs and tables or to 'finish off' the uprights of toilet mirrors, clock-cases, etc.

FLUTES Vertical concave channels, used as an additional ornament down chair legs, etc.

FRIEZE The surface below a cornice and the top-rails, immediately below the top of a table.

GADROONS A type of carving formed of convex curves (something like small bananas) appearing on mouldings on furniture.

GESSO The preparation of plaster or whiting used as the base to which gold leaf will adhere.

GOTHIC A name given to a style derived from Gothic architecture and principally used on furniture in the 15th and 16th Centuries. Came into use again in the middle of the 18th Century.

HAIR-CLAW Wood carved to represent a hairy claw foot.

KNEE The top part of a cabriole leg.

LINEN-FOLD A type of vertical carving that represents folded linen.

LONG-GRAIN MOULDING The moulding is worked with the grain running right along (not across) the moulding.

MARQUETRY The same designs cut in veneers of differing woods and fitted together.

MONOPODIUM A carved support for a table or chair with a lion-mask top.

MOULDINGS The edges of table-tops, cornices, etc, worked to give some emphasis or relief.

OGEE FOOT See bracket foot.

OPEN-FRET Fretwork that is pierced right through.

ORMOLU Gilt bronze ornament – usually used as mounts on furniture.

OVOLO MOULDING A moulding worked as a quarter curve – usually found on cornices.

OYSTERSHELL Wood used as a veneer that is cut across the branch of the tree and laid together to form a series of 'oysters'.

PAD The name given to the round foot at the base of a cabriole leg.

PATERA A round or oval decorative ornament carved or inlaid.

PATINA The undisturbed surface of wood that has been cared for and polished over a long period of time.

PIE-CRUST The name given to the moulded, scalloped and carved edge around a table-top – something like the fancy edge of a pastry pie.

POINTED TOE The name given to the pointed round foot at the base of a cabriole leg.

RABBET A groove cut lengthwise into which another piece of wood could be secured – sometimes drawer bottoms are so fixed, the bottoms fitted into the rabbet cut along the drawer side. Glasspanes are so fixed in bookcases.

REEDS Practically the opposite to flutes – vertical beads raised in relief as convex decoration on the legs of chairs and tables.

ROCOCO The name given to the style in the late part of the 18th Century. Lighter design, with slender curves, 'C' scrolls, foliage and flowers.

RULE-JOINT Usually to be found on flap tables when the joint of the flap is not square, shown best in the illustrations below.

RUNNER Someone who goes from house to house trying to buy pieces to sell to dealers; also, the strip of wood on which the drawer runs.

SCAGLIOLA A plaster or gesso top made to imitate marble – will take a very high polish.

SEAT-RAILS The framework of a chair seat.

SERPENTINE An in-and-out shape with a convex centre.

SPANDRELS Decoration confined to square corners – such as the usually pierced ornaments in the four corners of a clock dial.

SPLAT The upright central portion of a chair-back – whether solid, pierced or carved.

SPLIT BALUSTER A turned baluster split in half to form an applied ornament.

SPOKESHAVE A carpenter's tool for taking a thin shaving off a piece of wood.

SPOON-BACK When the solid splat of a chair curves somewhat like the handle of a spoon.

STRETCHER The piece of wood, sometimes square, sometimes moulded, that unites the legs of chairs or tables.

STRINGING Narrow lines of inlay of contrasting woods.

SUNBURST A shape like the sun's rays used as an inlay mainly between 1700–1720.

SWAG Very fashionable during the late 18th Century in Neo-Classic furniture, either as an inlaid shape or a similar carved shape like a festoon of flowers, or husks or laurels or drapery.

SWAN-NECK CORNICE When two sides of the cornice curve into scrolls each somewhat resembling a swan's neck.

TOP-RAIL The rail or piece of wood that joins the two back uprights at the top of the back of a chair, sometimes called cresting rail.

TURNING Turning in a lathe to produce rounded shapes.

VENEER Thin pieces of wood, formerly cut by hand, sometimes as much as $\frac{1}{8}''$ thick. Nowadays it is cut by machines and is much thinner.

Its object was to produce a decorative effect—very pretty wood being cut into veneers: mahogany, yew, mulberry, tulipwood, rosewood, kingwood, walnut, laburnum, etc.

Index

Italic figures refer to plate numbers